Who Stole Your Rainbow?

Simple steps to heal your mind

Who Stole Your Rainbow?

Simple steps to heal your mind

Danusha Chandrasekaran

PAPER TOWNS
PUBLISHERS

PAPER TOWNS
PUBLISHERS

First published by
Papertowns Publishers
72, Vishwanath Dham Colony,
Niwaru Road, Jhotwara,
Jaipur, 302012

Who Stole Your Rainbow?

ISBN Print Book - 978-93-91228-32-3

Cover visualization: Danusha
Cover design/illustration: Creative Factory
www.creativefactory.lk

This is my samarpanam to Thatha.

K.T.M Karuppiah Pillai

After my dad passed away, he was the one constant in my life who taught me the importance of discipline in daily living, and how simplicity, generosity and kindness can impact the lives of the people around us.

Also

Have you found your happy place

Reviews for Have you found your happy place

As a teacher I enjoyed every page of the book, as it helped me take a leaf out of it to engage my students with the values and equivalent quotations. The author Danusha Chandrasekaran has conscientiously put it together ensuring that all ages would enjoy and benefit from the same. Waiting for the second book substance.

Geetha Sundar
HOD English
The PSBBMILLENNIUM School
Chennai

Have you Found your Happy Place is a fascinating compilation of beautiful, impactful and most apt quotes from some of the most renowned authors from across the world. It has covered so many varied subjects that certainly leads us many steps closer to finding ourself. And what's definitely the highlight is Danusha Chandrasekaran's wonderful afterthoughts regarding the same subjects that brings those words to life by simplifying them for just anyone to read including my 9yr old daughter Geena. I truly look forward to getting my hands on her next treasure trove of encouragement and insight.

Inez Parris
English Language/ IELTS/ PTE Trainer
Pune

In this bright little book brimming with thoughts for the day, quotes and messages, the author Danusha Chandrasekaran brings to the reader an individual secret path to their happy place.

Each page carries a message and each reader will find their way through this book. I tend to randomly open to a page believing that the message will be the right advice for me on that day and often it appears to be. Some readers may prefer to read a page a day but it's not the kind of book to finish and put away in your bookshelf. Instead, it's something to leave by your bedside to read, reflect and meditate on the meaning of the words on the page, on the philosophy of life and on living.

Not every path is easy and some suggestions, although important such as those 'on forgiveness' and letting go may prove difficult to many. However, owning and reading this first book with its bright and attractive front cover will set many readers on the path to finding their happy place.

It's my fervent hope there will soon be another book by this budding authoress brimming with self-knowledge shared with her readers. Furthermore, her next book will surely provide the reader with the tools they require to carve their own happy place.
Wishing every success to Danusha

Dr Sharmila Khot
Consultant in Anaesthesia and Pain Medicine
Cardiff and Vale University Health Board
United Kingdom

It is a tiny book if you look at the number pages and the author's first book; but the content was designed so nicely that anyone can read any page at any time. The author had put in her thoughts in delivering the message so clearly and direct to the point that the readers can easily understand without much interpretation. This is the key difference, which makes it handier for readers of any background. Generally, the common belief is that self-motivation books are more for office goers; but this book is designed keeping all people in mind; we can recommend for anyone, irrespective of profession, age and background.

I wish the author all the best and I'm looking forward to seeing the next book.

G. Soundararajan
Lead Solutions Architect (IT)
Yoga & Meditation teacher
Singapore

Danusha Chandrasekaran's 'Have you found your Happy Place- Daily Reminders to oneself' is a motivational book aimed for all ages. The entire tiny book exemplifies positivity and heart-felt vibrations.

The golden quotes focused on the main muse of the author's intension in writing the book, reasons which cause life to be worthwhile.

Really, I am decisively convinced that everyone instinctively knows how to repair themselves.

The quotes have multiplicity views of life. The author's in-depth ideas are great; it is definitely worth a read, even to a grown-up audience.

Prof.
N. Senthil Kumaran,
Director,
Computer Applications,
Vellalar College of Women (Autonomous), Erode.

Acknowledgements

I like knowing that we cannot exist on our own. The Universe keeps us all under her umbrella, connecting us with like-minded souls. Every person we meet are in our lives for a reason. That's why life is filled with intricate joys. Everyone is a teacher, only we need to be ready to learn from them all.

In spirituality, the emphasis on having a Guru is laid. There is a common refrain; when the student is ready the master appears. My SadhGuru Sai entered my life at an opportune moment, paving way for a multifold of miracles to happen.

We cannot progress unless we have mentors and I owe my gratitude to Ms. Dimple Anil, who infused in me immense inner strength. She instilled courage and confidence and, like a child in kindergarten, I relearnt the basics on the kind and just way of leading a righteous life. She taught me to Trust My Trust.

My parents have been the reason for my love of reading from a very young age. My dad, N.P. Shanmugam and my mom, Bhavani, ensured that I always had a steady supply of books, thereby ensuring that I lived in a world full of dreams and possibilities.

I truly wouldn't know what I would do without my three musketeers. My husband Chandrasekaran and my sons Adhiinthran and Dheexshan encompass my whole world and effectively, complete me.

There are people and then there are special people. My friends are my special people. They have been an immense source of strength to me, and with them as my support system, there is absolutely no room for failure.

I owe a lot to my dearest friend Leena. She is my friend, philosopher and guide. I can never do justice to her unconditional belief in me. She supports my dreams to the extent of gifting me all the books I want, knowing how much I value and need them. While her passion for reading matches mine, her generosity exceeds that of mine, in ways unfathomable. Kindness, I learnt, is wanting only the best for others unconditionally.

To Inez, I will forever be indebted. Not everyone can encourage or literally help someone start from the very bottom, but Inez believed in my vision, my passion and my dreams. She ensured that success was within my reach, which laid the foundation for Serenity to blossom and take off.

I am immensely grateful to my brother Dharshan. He weaves my dreams into beautiful realities. From designing this book cover to all of Serenity's visuals, he is a creative wizard.

I owe a huge thanks to my elder brother Dinesh for being an epitome of goodness. I have been the recipient of his innumerable acts of kindness and he is my voice of calm amidst all chaos.

To my friends Dr Sharmila and Dr Shailaja, a simple thank you will never suffice. I am lucky to be travelling with them in this lifetime because they lead exemplary lives. They taught me the true spirit of living to one's truest potential and have been the people I look up to. I am humbled by the foreword and reviews and it makes me want to do even better.

I feel immensely blessed to have connected with Manik and Paper Towns publishing. Manik has literally been guiding me every step of the way. If I say my learning curve was enormous it would be an understatement. It was gigantic. Thank you, team Paper Towns. I also owe Shivang a special thanks for making my life that much easier.

At Serenity, every reader is family. They walk alongside me every single day. They give me the impetus to strive for the best and to keep providing motivational content of high standards. They inspire me to turn up and they are equally responsible for all my successes. I will always be in gratitude to them all.

If I am able to string all these words together, it is because of the inspiration I get from all authors. I like to think that I have learnt, am learning and will learn only from the best because of these wise souls. They have taught me to raise my quality of thinking and left in me their indelible impression that will last this lifetime and next.

Contents

My story....1
Aspiring to dream....4
Goals and goal settings....6
Why forgiveness needs to be an integral part of one's life?....8
Decluttering....12
10 minutes towards a better you....14
The need for mentors....16
Healing....19
Writing down prayers....21
"Dare to be"....23
Mistakes....24
How do I wake up to a new day?....26
Feelings....28
Nice but not nice....30
Words as currencies....32
There is no point in carrying the past....34
The invitation....36
The words we speak....40
Energy and its significance....43
Disassociating with others' opinions....46
The strangest secret....48

We are all connected 50
When in love 52
Complaining in times of calamity 54
How to be happy 56
Are you on a diet? 58
Introspection and conquering our weaknesses 60
Who stole your rainbow? 63
How to handle anxiousness? 66
Gossip 69
Don't take everything personally 71
Give yourself permission to be happy 73
Be true to yourself 74
Life 76
Bamboo and fern 78
What can I do for you? 81
What will it take for you to live life to your fullest potential? 82
You are not your thoughts 84
The excuses we always come up with. 87
When my mind says why? 89
Emotional upheaval and rebuilding 91
The gift of time 93
Focus on what you want, not on what you don't want 96
Your choices lead the way. 99
The bundle of misery 101
Toxic relationships 103
Outlook 105
The power of silence 107
The stories you never hear. 109
If I can 111
Affirmations 113
Desiderata- words for life 116
Our truest freedom comes from our fight from within 119

Success is not in your failure it's in your never say die attitude....122
To thine own self be true. 124
Don't quit 126
What can't be taken away from you 128
Learn to let go 130
Reclaim your power 132
Looping thoughts....134
Are you holding onto guilt?....136
Thank you 138
Conclusion 140
Quotations....143

Foreword

It gives me immense pleasure to write this foreword for Ms. Danusha Chandrasekaran's second book, ***Who stole your Rainbow?***

I was first introduced to Danusha's E-Magazine, *Serenity,* by my medical school friend in early 2021. A Psychiatrist myself, I have always been drawn to read stories about personal growth and development.

As you can imagine, early 2021 was different. All of us, Global Citizens have been affected by the recent SARS2, COVID-19 pandemic that took the world by intense shock in 2020 and continued into 2021.

There isn't a single person I know who has not been touched on a personal and deeper level by the pandemic - most people lost someone or knew of someone who died of the corona virus. These are especially challenging times, with loss of human lives, jobs, finances, relationships, and worsening health co-morbidities. These were times when most people found themselves introspecting, and making changes to the way they lived and went about their daily lives. How could we not? We became much more aware of what really mattered on a daily basis. Many decided to leave their work and retire early, or start working for themselves or do what their heart had always desired.

It was at this time, that I decided to subscribe to *Serenity*. I am happy I did; I look forward to starting my day with an uplifting message from Danusha, and that would set the tone for the rest of my day. I wonder how Danusha comes up with a message that always seems like it was written just for me! Ms. Danusha Chandrasekaran has the perfect qualifications and life experience with a Masters in Human Development and Family Studies, which has given her the utmost ability to give forward to the world tools and practices that change the way each one of us can find our true authentic selves.

I had the opportunity to read Danusha's first publication, *Have you found your happy place,* in the summer of 2021. It is not a book that the reader must read cover to cover - it's your choice! I found myself opening the book and reading the 1-2 pages I happened to open the book to, and after reading it, I'd take some time to introspect and reflect. Every time I read or re-read the book, I'd come away with a deeper meaning to the quote, the affirmation, the passage, or the explanation. What I again was awe struck about, was how beautifully Danusha had gathered so many rich sources, famous authors, writers and their meaningful writings and then elaborated on them in her own way in this book. I found it extremely easy to read and more importantly, so meaningful just when I needed it. Danusha is talented and gifted with the ability to use words and give them a deeper and more positive meaning, and her writing just flows, enticing the reader to read the book in its entirety.

In *Who Stole Your Rainbow,* Danusha has aptly put together, in lovely meaningful prose, chapters that approach life lessons for anyone and everyone. If you are on the path of finding your Inner Self, or want to get more meaning out of your life, or if you are a curious reader, I am convinced that each one of you will find a message that will strike a chord for you and you will return to Danusha's book to find pearls of wisdom that you will be able to put into practice. Her writings and vignettes will leave you with tools to problem solve in your relationships, your work, and daily lives. You will come away with the ability to shift your perspective so that you are left feeling much more empowered and ready to take on the World!

I wish Ms. Danusha Chandrasekaran much success as she continues to help the world live a fuller, more meaningful and authentic life by utilizing her gift with words and her experience in the mental health field.

Best wishes

Shailaja Shah, MD
Board Certified Psychiatrist
Hackensack Meridian health- Carrier clinic
New Jersey, USA

My story

I have always wanted to write. My love for words and my passion to write was something I inculcated while growing up in an English convent boarding school, and my earliest memory began with writing poems on tiny scraps of paper I came across. I continued scribbling on random sheets and participated in writing contests while in college. It was more of an obsession, where I sought avenues to express my thoughts. I have never regretted being a homemaker because I always put my kids before me, and being there for them mattered more to me, far more than pursuing my dreams. I would spend my days happily reading, which was rewarding in its own way. I firmly believe that the Universe always has plans for everyone. It is wiser that way. I had made a request to the Universe sharing my dreams and hopes. The Universe decided to nudge me along with courses, mentors, friends and family who guided me, taking me step by step, towards my goals.

Experience was my best teacher. It taught me who my friends were and the lessons I needed to learn. It taught me to fail and to succeed, how to trust and how to heal. I have learnt the impermanence of it all.

I have only the deepest gratitude for the people who tore into my very essence, and for breaking my faith and trust. If not for them, I would have been just another ordinary person. I am truly grateful for all my stumbling blocks, for all the people who didn't value what I offered. It made me much more determined in finding new ways to grow higher.

Today I can confidently radiate love, warmth and hope. I can instill confidence in people who seek my help. I can reach out to many because I know what it is to be on the side of despair. I know how a wounded heart will hurt. I know how silence can seem like heaven. I know how it is to cry deep into a pillow so that sounds don't reach out. How the tears don't fall while your mouth refuses to open and when pain is so numbing and you are entrenched deep within yourself, safe, that no one can reach inside your deepest core.

This journey is one of courage. Of standing up for oneself. Of letting the critics do what they do best. To keep criticizing as you keep soaring. The one thing that has also kept me grounded was my amazing family. I am nothing without them. The same applies to my friends. I keep my circle very small. What they have done for me is nothing in comparison to what I do. For all of these divine mercies I am truly grateful.

Let these words speak to you, dear reader. May they touch a chord. May you know that you are not alone. May you have the wisdom to make good choices. May you have the strength to pursue them. May the Divine be your guiding light.

I asked myself what it was, that I could share, so that when you are done reading this book, you either have a smile on your face or are left reflecting on what you just read. What will add value to your life? And it just clicked. In an instant, I knew I had the answer. If I can share the different slices of life on the problems faced by real people, you would resonate with it.

I firmly believe that each person is endowed with a unique talent. We just need to unearth it. My talent has always been my words. I was the go-to counsellor for many people. People approached me seeking help and guidance insisting that my words were healing them. I knew then, that this was my purpose, and I think everyone needs to find their true purpose. Shouldn't we all try to leave this earth a much better place than before? Everyone has a unique way of doing it and that's why this journey is all the more beautiful. We all bring our different personalities to make this world a wonderful place to live in.

I began my journey offering nuggets of wisdom to friends who were in desperate need of them. They asked, and I complied. But we know experience can be a gamechanger. I upgraded my skillsets to be of better service to the same people who needed me, but this time, with confidence. Serenity was my way of helping people rewire their way of thinking. Having meaningful, spiritual practices empowered me to reach out to more people, and therein began a wonderful journey. It's not been an easy road. But it's definitely been rewarding to the core.

Aspiring to dream

"If one advances confidently in the direction of one's dreams, and endeavours to live the life which one has imagined, one will meet with a success unexpected in common hours." – Henry David Thoreau

Having a dream is the first step towards success. As Walt Disney said "If you can dream it, you can do it."

My policy in life is to do all that I love. To indulge in my creative pursuits. To push boundaries and test my limitations.

I like knowing I tried before I gave up. If I am always going to let the opinions of others be my benchmark for wanting to succeed, I will be like a bird with clipped wings.

I would rather break my wings dashing them against the mountains I try soaring above from, rather than handing someone a pair of scissors to clip them before I fly.

There are no big dreams or small dreams. As long as it's mine, that's all that counts.

I want to be known for the things I did rather than for the dreams that failed to materialize due to doubts and fears.

Was I scared before I tried something new?

Yes. The doubts, fears and self-criticism were dramatic.

Did I continue? Of course, I knew I would only feel more upset if I didn't take that chance.

Am I famous? Not yet.

Will I be? Why Not.

I am that tiny miniscule speck in this vast wide world, hoping to make a difference nano particle by nano particle... Word by word.

I learnt that we can never measure ourselves against another's success but we can surely measure it by the effort and dedication we put in making our dreams come true.

Goals and goal settings

"A person should set his goals as early as he can and devote all his energy and talent to getting there. With enough effort, he may achieve it. Or he may find something that is even more rewarding. But in the end, no matter what the outcome, he will know he has been alive." –Walt Disney

The process of setting goals helps you choose where you want to go in life. By knowing precisely what you want to achieve, you know where you have to concentrate your efforts. You'll also quickly spot the distractions that can, so easily, lead you astray.

While setting up a goal, motivation isn't enough to get you through. You initially commence with great intentions and excitement and you tend to be committed. After the initial buzz fades, monotony hits in and boredom sets in.

Your mind brings up a whole gamut of questions. Do I have to do this every day? It's so boring.

I want to sleep for just 5 more minutes. Let's compromise on the snack. It's just a tiny piece.

My body is aching. I will skip my exercise routine just for one day.

Your excuses become real to you and you convince yourself of how it doesn't matter as much.

Initially, if it seems too much, try half-sized goals. If you're struggling to attain a goal that seems to be too challenging, set a less difficult version of the goal. Break it down to micro habits. It's always advisable to start tackling the easier and smaller goals and then work upwards. If you're not getting good results, you can always go back and tweak what you're doing. Don't feel compelled to change everything in your life, all at once.

Truth is; it's just a practice. You don't overthink. You just do, and keep on repeating. As and when you keep on doing something, it becomes a habit that you don't think about anymore. For instance, brushing your teeth. It is a daily habit, and you don't think about doing it. You just do it. You don't have to exert yourself to brush.

Developing habits is similar and becomes ingrained in you. In a while, before you realize, you just start doing it all.

Why forgiveness needs to be an integral part of one's life?

> *It can be hard to forgive and let go but it's important to remember that harbouring the resentment and holding a grudge can hurt you even more. The word "forgive" really means to give something up for YOURSELF – not for them. – Jack Canfield*

If there is one sensitive topic, it would be this; Forgiveness. Or to put it more succinctly, the importance of forgiving and the absolute necessity in doing so.

In my interactions with varied people, I found this to be a common occurrence amongst many. They were hurt by the actions of their loved ones and they had absolutely no clue on how to overcome them.

We have all been hurt by someone, maybe recently or maybe eons ago. But we still carry it with us because it has lodged its way deep within. Our scars run too deep because we feel betrayed. Where loved ones are involved, the hurt is not easy to let go. Our emotional connect with them breaks into our very essence and all that we stood for.

We spend disproportionate amount of our time and energies wishing for the pain to go away, trying to rewrite the incidents in our minds, and even spend a fair deal of it in unburdening our sorrows to the people around us, hoping we will get the solace we need.

How does someone get off this emotional mess one is entangled in? How do we raise our vibration? What exactly is one supposed to do next?

Forgiveness can seem unnatural as our sense of righteousness insists that people should pay for the wrongs they committed.

Only when we are able to forgive, are we able to move forward in life. No matter how many times we hear the oft repeated statement that states, 'holding onto anger is like drinking poison', hoping the other person dies, we need to hear it again.

The path to forgiveness is rocky and filled with trepidations. It will be the hardest journey we take. But taking the path of least resistance is more harmful than beneficial in the long run. We understand an essential truth that no one can rescue us from this pain. This is a continuous and ongoing process where we work on ourselves step by step, day by day.

Resentments and past hurt cripple us and don't allow us to progress. In order to move forward, we will have to cut these chains. Practice detaching yourself mentally from the person and the situation. Set intentions where you can release people with peace and love. You make a conscious choice to disassociate with the negativity. There's just no easy way about it. It is an integral part of one's daily routine.

Forgive the people who hurt you. Most of all, forgive yourself. Sometimes it's comparatively easy to forgive others while we still feel guilty for what we have done.

Forgive yourself for it's the only way you come unstuck. Remember you did the best you could with the mind frame you were in.

Spirituality taught me certain truths.

Practicing forgiveness helps release the past. It doesn't mean one forgets or condones what transpired, but it's a conscious choice to release its hold on your life.

There are some people we meet and interact with on a daily basis. The power is in not letting them run our day and ruin it.

There is wisdom in understanding that the powers above, always knew what my circumstances were at all times and how to deal with all the people beyond my limitations.

My job was to be the best person I possibly could and not worry about why certain people behaved in a certain way.

I ask myself if I have full control of my thought and emotions. Which were the areas I was lacking in, and what I intended to do about it. I ask myself if I am disciplined and if I can complete the plans that I set out to do.

I shift my focus and energies and redirect them productively, engaging in tasks that I am completely involved in, those that make me happy and those that keep me occupied.

I consciously disconnect with the thoughtforms that bring up memories of past incidents or hurt.

I chose to do my forgiveness prayers on a continuous basis and I didn't just stop with forgiveness. I blessed them all.

As healers we are taught varied techniques to disintegrate the negative energies, but to do that, we need to be in an elevated state of vibration. We need to have been regular in spiritual practices.

But I found that the simplest tool available to every lay person was to use intentions. We set clear intentions of disconnecting our energies from those whom we don't have a good relationship with. We shift our focus from all the negativity and think of all the good we can. Though it may seem difficult initially, as is the case with all practices, it becomes second nature. You will be able to interact with the same people and be unaffected by them because you are now vibrating on a completely higher plane.

Jack Canfield's forgiveness affirmation "I release myself from all the demands and judgments that have kept me limited. I allow myself to go free – to live in joy and love and peace. I allow myself to create fulfilling relationships, to have success in my life, to experience peace, to know that I am worthy and deserve to have what I want. I now go free. In that process I release all others from any demands and expectations I have placed on them. I choose to be free. I allow others to be free. I forgive myself and I forgive them. And so, it is."

Decluttering

"Every minute you spend looking through clutter, wondering where you put this or that, being unable to focus because you're not organized costs you: time you could have spent with family or friends, time you could have been productive around the house, time you could have been making money." – Jean Chatzky

Clutter is anything that you are holding onto, which doesn't add value to your life. Decluttering is respecting and taking care of yourself by letting go of the things that you have accumulated and no longer need.

Having clean and clear spaces makes way for a better way of living. When you clean, tidy and declutter your home, your mental, emotional and physical wellbeing is automatically enhanced and it doesn't have to be overwhelming. When you don't practice mindful living, you often leave a lot of mess for other people to clear up.

Organizing and decluttering relieves stress for many people by providing a sense of control and accomplishment.

If you are new to decluttering, start by taking micro steps.

Decide on one area you want to focus on, and use that as your starting point as you go from room to room, clearing spaces.

Return everything to its original place. Later, when you are in a better frame of mind, you can start sorting through your stuff.

Before you go to bed at night, ensure that there's nothing out of its place.

This ensures, in the morning when you wake up, you wake up to clean spaces.

A small trick you can apply is that, every time you walk through a room and find things out of place, take them with you and return them to their original place.

The less things you have outside, the more peace you will get.

Find a place for the things that can go into cupboards and keep them there, instead of having them all over the place.

Donate and recycle what you can, and dump what you don't want anymore.

Take help from your family or friends when you need help with disposing things.

An exercise you can try is, to leave no trace behind of your presence. Whenever you leave a room, ensure that everything is straightened up, leaving no trace that you occupied that space.

Apply the 30-day rule or 60 or 90 or any number of days that you want, that you think you can adhere to. Every day, dispose one item you don't want. You will be free of those many items and you will realize you aren't missing them anymore.

10 minutes towards a better you

"When you take care of yourself, you're a better person for others. When you feel good about yourself, you treat others better." —Solange Knowles

10 minutes. That's all it takes. How can 10 minutes add value to my life?

Seriously? You have got to be kidding me... (Is that your voice that I hear?) ...

Well, being put like this, it either sounds way too easy or way too hard for some.

But, let me break it down for you...

10 minutes per day is 60 minutes in 6 days. 25 hours takes 150 days and on an average 5 months.

So, in five months, you will definitely no longer be where you started from.

You would be comparatively more skilled than you are right now.

Apply this rule in any area of your life, to acquire a new skill or to strengthen an existing one.

The key is doing it every day for 10 minutes.

Initially it's easy to follow habits if you have a routine time.

You need to go through your daily schedule and find consistent pockets of time and stick to doing it at that particular time.

James Clear, in his book Atomic Habits, stated that on average, it takes more than 2 months before a new behaviour becomes automatic — 66 days to be exact. And how long it takes a new habit to form can vary widely, depending on the behaviour, the person, and the circumstances. In Lally's study, it took anywhere from 18 days to 254 days for people to form a new habit.

In other words, if you want to set your expectations appropriately, the truth is that it will probably take you anywhere from two months to eight months to build a new behaviour into your life — not 21 days. Take time to think about what you want to do. Push yourself to take up something that you are lagging behind on, or hesitant to try. You can apply it to personal development, skill building, conquering your fears or for going after your dreams.

The need for mentors

"The mind is not a vessel that needs filling, but wood that needs igniting." – Plutarch

A mentor is someone with knowledge and experience and a person who will help you improve your skills, make better decisions and throw light on the new perspectives required by you in your desired field. They're willing to share this knowledge with you in order to help you achieve your goals. A mentor should be someone who has achieved the level of success that you envision for yourself. It's someone who can challenge you and push you in ways other people can't. Rather than learning the hard way and navigating through trial and error, a mentor is a person you can look to for direction, in addition being a role model to imitate.

Do you wish to be successful? Here is a story that teaches you how to apply the wisdom of ancient world to the practical world of today

This story was written by Derek Lin, an award-winning bestselling author in the Tao genre and highlights the importance of having a mentor.

A young man once worked in a factory, and had an old technician for a mentor who taught him various techniques to develop his skills. When the old technician retired ten years later, the young man became a technician himself and continued to work with dedication. One day, he visited his mentor, who noticed the young man was unhappy. On being asked the reason behind this unhappiness, the man replied, "I have been following your instructions all these years. Although I have done good work, the people who do not have my experience or capabilities have been promoted, while I am making as little as I did before."

The old man asks the young man if he has become indispensable to the factory, to which the young man nods his head. The mentor advises him to take a break, after which the young man is promoted as a senior technician by the manager since the factory faces problems in his absence. The young man repeats this trick time and again, and eventually loses his job. He rushes to the mentor and realizes he had heard only half of his mentor's advice.

"Nobody notices a light bulb that is always on. Only the day it goes off is when people suddenly start noticing it", said the mentor. "However,", he said, stressing on the most important part of the lesson, "if a light bulb goes off frequently, it is replaced by a more reliable one." This story shares the wisdom of the ancient and helps us understand how to achieve success in the current world.

Mentors play an important role in a person's life. They provide knowledge and encouragement, help you become a much better and improved version of yourself and help you avoid the pitfalls by sharing experiences. Having a mentor assures a person that they are on the right track provided they have a good mentor who knows and understands them. This can be a transformational learning and growth experience.

Healing

"I have come to understand that some of the deepest and most effective healing is not found at a doctor's office or a hospital, but rather from inside ourselves. Our bodies are designed for self-healing, and we are capable of both boosting and blocking that ability."
– Dr. Daju Suzanne Friedman

The reality of healing is we have to go through the whole process of disintegration before we become whole again. We combust and it feels like we have been burnt to ashes. But we forget, that within us all, is the Phoenix waiting to rise again.

When life hits us hard, when we face betrayal, when hearts get broken, it can all seem too distressing. But one needs to remember that healing is process. It's a process of wanting to get better and believing that there is a way out of all the messes we are caught up in.

The first step to healing is acknowledging that there exists a problem. Second, is believing in oneself to know that hardships can be overcome. Moreover, even though we have a very good support system, what each person goes through is extremely personal, and we have to trust ourselves completely, truly believing that we are brave enough to withstand what life throws at us.

But the beauty of having a support system is that there will be people whom you can lean on, at least till you catch your breath, before continuing on your journey.

And the most beautiful thing about any kind of healing, is that when you evolve, you shine like a star.

You emerge much stronger, much more compassionate and you become a beacon of hope to others. Your empathy makes you a people magnet. You become the voice of reason and a ray of sunshine whom people seek out.

Writing down prayers

When you feel like worrying, try praying instead. Worrying only creates more stress, but prayer creates more peace. God is bigger than whatever is stressing you out." – Dave Willis

Writing prayers is a form of meditation. It's peaceful, soothing and completely relaxing. It's equivalent to taking that first sip of tea. It's being in the moment where you, your prayers and the silence around is all that you are aware of.

Sometimes when you're praying internally, you would have noticed your mind drifting. The act of physically writing out your prayer forces you to stay focused on the next word, the next sentence and the purpose behind your writing.

That deeper focus often leads to a more personal view of God. The thoughts that might have drifted off when praying internally are all of a sudden staring at you from the page. Not only are your words visible, but your relationship is, too. When done with utter focus, writing down prayers becomes magical in its own way, since every word you write feels like your private conversation with God.

You can write your very own prayers or you can copy them from the words of your holy books or your Gurus. Just be conscious that it isn't some meaningless activity. Ensure you take in each word and be mindful of what you are writing down. Writing down prayers can be extremely therapeutic and like any mindfulness practice, it should be slow and you should be completely aware of what you write.

If you feel inspired to write prayers, then go ahead and write, it can be an uplifting exercise. It is simply the act of taking words and using them carefully to express your own thoughts and feelings.

"Dare to be"

By Steve Maraboli

When a new day begins, dare to smile gratefully.
When there is darkness, dare to be the first to shine a light.
When there is injustice, dare to be the first to condemn it.
When something seems difficult, dare to do it anyway.
When life seems to beat you down, dare to fight back.
When there seems to be no hope, dare to find some.
When you're feeling tired, dare to keep going.
When times are tough, dare to be tougher.
When love hurts you, dare to love again.
When someone is hurting, dare to help them heal.
When another is lost, dare to help them find the way.
When a friend falls, dare to be the first to extend a hand.
When you cross paths with another, dare to make them smile.
When you feel great, dare to help someone else feel great too.
When the day has ended, dare to feel as you've done
your best.
Dare to be the best you can –
At all times, Dare to be!"

Mistakes

"We are all flawed. Every one of us. And believe me, we've all made mistakes. You've just got to take a good hard look at yourself, change what needs to be changed, and move on." – Lauren Myracle

Life is all about the goof ups. Imagine if you never made a mistake. How boring is that? Also, how will learning ever happen if everyone traversed the same path. Mistakes are a part and parcel of life. We slip up, get up and slip up again. Every time we get up, we learn. Being down is not an option.

There's no foolishness in making mistakes and learning from them.

Sometimes people make you feel ashamed and guilty when you have committed a mistake.

But mistakes are beautiful. Because it is only there, when your true potential for growth begins.

Only if you repeatedly do the same thing, can you be called foolish. At times your heart is too tender and your trust immense, and you let yourself think that things will change, or maybe the person will. You hold onto hope.

But with all tough lessons come immense personal growth.

Behind every successful person is the story of all their hardships and all that they overcame.

Each of our stories maybe different. But the path we all seek is always goodness.

In achieving that, we achieve success.

How do I wake up to a new day?

"Every morning, when we wake up, we have twenty-four brand new hours to live. What a precious gift! We have the capacity to live in a way that these twenty-four hours will bring peace, joy, and happiness to ourselves and others." – Thich Nhat Hanh

Every day is a gift from the Divine. We are all given 24 hours to have a brand-new start.

A day to fulfil our dreams while creating new ones; to achieve our goals and be proactive. A day filled with happiness and warmth.

A day well begun is a day half done. When we start off with the right mindset, we set the tone for the rest of the day.

We give ourselves the impetus to achieve more, making our day a productive and a happy one.

So how does one ensure a good start?

A new day always begins with a smile. Before you step out of bed; smile. Recollect a few incidents that make you smile and you will automatically find yourself smiling.

Practice gratitude. For all the things you have and for all that you are about to receive.

Take time to sit in quiet contemplation. Reflect on all the good you are surrounded with. It assures you of peace and stillness.

Drink that glass of warm water. Hydrate. Do this to stimulate your organs.

Read or recite your daily prayers. Be one with the Divine. You can do Affirmations, Mantra chanting, visualization.

Do light stretches, yoga or walking. Do Tai chi or Qigong. Physical movement provides the needed circulation.

Be in nature. It makes you more appreciative of the wonders of the universe and can boost your mood.

Be present and in the moment. The key to happiness lies in focusing more on the present rather than spending time recalling and thinking of the past.

The quality of our lives is determined by the quality of our thoughts.

Marcus Aurelius said "When you arise in the morning, think of what a precious privilege it is to be alive – to breathe, to think, to enjoy, to love."

Feelings

"The emotion that can break your heart is sometimes the very one that heals it" – Nicholas Sparks

Do you know what it feels like to be a tightly wound string...?

So tight that you know one pull and every link will break

You feel the glass shattering into a million pieces

In a world of your own, you make your path

Where you hold everything within

Knowing that neither screaming nor shouting will help you

Every crevice within can hear your innermost thoughts, your tears and your despair

Yet, you know that being strong is the only way forward

You despise a lot of things

The ugliness of petty-minded people

You get sullied by their gossips and negative thoughts

You are at a point where walking away might seem like bliss

Reality sets in and being strong is the only way to go

Don't hold back. Don't be this way...

Your mind might convince your heart

But the poor thing has too much to take and it closes in.

It's a tough world out there

And being a dreamer is an escape route...

You safely time travel to places where you can weave your own stories

Stories of happiness, stories that bring a smile

If that isn't to be so.... Life would become unbearable

Do what works to ignite your mind and spark your joys.

Nice, but not nice

"Believing you're a good person and actually being one are two completely different things." —Anonymous

There are different people you meet;

Your friends, acquaintances, relations and at times it could even be close family.

The ones who are good are easy to handle

They are your people

The ones you share a laugh with; keeper of your secrets

They become your shoulders and arms when you need a hug

Then there are the sandwich people

They are neither here nor there

You neither have a great relationship nor a bitter one

Like seasons, they just pass you by

Like spring, summer, autumn and winter

You either enjoy their company or you don't pay them much heed

Then come the game changers

The nice people but just not your people

The ones who persist in making your life challenging

Rather than giving them power and spending time proving, they make your life miserable

You take ownership of your power.

You label them interesting and creative

Because they sure do know which buttons to push and when

It's like you need to be alert at all times so you don't say a wrong word

Come to think of it, these people are the ones who actually bring out the best in you

They teach you to be better versions of yourselves

They are the role models of how you shouldn't be

You learn how to dig deeper and find reservoirs of strength you never knew you had

You learn patience, tolerance and empathy

You learn from your weaknesses and you learn to forgive more

To all those who push your buttons

Thank them for making you stronger

Thank them for coming into your life and teaching you, your much-needed lessons

Thank them for always reminding you that though you may slip up, you're always going to get back up.

And when you get up, you are going to be stronger than before.

Words as currencies

"Be mindful when it comes to your words. A string of some that don't mean much to you, may stick with someone else for a lifetime." – Rachel Wolchin

Imagine if we were told that words are currencies.

We have been given an unlimited access to this resource.

We can spend it to our hearts liking without ever fearing it would run out.

But there's a catch.

Like every financial year, an audit would happen.

All the good you spoke, thought, and did would return back to you with interest.

Whereas everything else would be deducted.

You will have penalties in the form of unrest, illness, unhappiness, sadness, worries and tensions.

Now, would you be more careful with your words or even more careless?

We have all become a product of mindless actions.

They are so ingrained in the way we live that we don't even realize where it is that we are going wrong.

People always say, 'we live only once'. The truth is, we die only once. We live every single day.

We have a chance to turn things around every single day.

We have innumerable learnings and lessons to learn every single day.

An idle mind is a devil's workshop. A conscious mind is an abode for the Divine.

There is no point in carrying the past

"We are products of our past, but we don't have to be prisoners of it." –Rick Warren

"The past is like a cancelled cheque. It has no value. It is futile to keep brooding over past worries, hurts and pains, in effect making the present miserable."

Once a disciple went to his spiritual master and cried, "Guruji, I have so many difficulties and pains in my heart that I have been carrying from the past and I could not get rid of them. Please help me to attain mental peace."

The guru gave him various spiritual advices but the disciple could not grasp them well and put them into practice; he continued to suffer from the thoughts of the past and he kept complaining to the Guru again and again.

Then, the Guru gave him a sack load of vegetables weighing about 15 kilos and said to the disciple, "You carry this on your shoulders all the time; even when you are lying down for resting or sleeping, you should hold it on your chest. Do this till I give further instructions".

The disciple obeyed the guru and carried the sack load of vegetables all the time on his shoulders or on his head. It was very painful and tiring for him. During nights, he kept the sack on his chest and slept. He could not sleep well.

He kept on doing this for the next few days. The vegetables started decaying and soon a foul smell started emanating from the sack. As they decayed further, liquid started dripping from the sack, which he found extremely irritating and itchy.

Unable to bear the pain and discomfort any longer, he ran to the guru and sought his permission to throw away the burden. The Guru gave his permission and said, "This is precisely what I was advising you with regard to your carrying the mental burden of the past too! That too, was heavy, painful, irritating and itching in your mind! If only you could throw them away like the sack that you did now, you will be relieved!"

The invitation

Oriah Mountain Dreamer

It doesn't interest me
what you do for a living.
I want to know
what you ache for
and if you dare to dream
of meeting your heart's longing.

It doesn't interest me
how old you are.
I want to know
if you will risk
looking like a fool
for love
for your dream
for the adventure of being alive.

It doesn't interest me
what planets are
squaring your moon...
I want to know
if you have touched

the centre of your own sorrow
if you have been opened
by life's betrayals
or have become shrivelled and closed
from fear of further pain.

I want to know
if you can sit with pain
mine or your own
without moving to hide it
or fade it
or fix it.

I want to know
if you can be with joy
mine or your own
if you can dance with wildness
and let the ecstasy fill you
to the tips of your fingers and toes
without cautioning us
to be careful
to be realistic
to remember the limitations
of being human.

It doesn't interest me
if the story you are telling me
is true.
I want to know if you can
disappoint another
to be true to yourself.
If you can bear
the accusation of betrayal
and not betray your own soul.

If you can be faithless
and therefore trustworthy.

I want to know if you can see beauty
even when it is not pretty
every day.
And if you can source your own life
from its presence.

I want to know
if you can live with failure
yours and mine
and still stand at the edge of the lake
and shout to the silver of the full moon,
"Yes."

It doesn't interest me
to know where you live
or how much money you have.
I want to know if you can get up
after the night of grief and despair
weary and bruised to the bone
and do what needs to be done
to feed the children.

It doesn't interest me
who you know
or how you came to be here.
I want to know if you will stand
in the centre of the fire
with me
and not shrink back.

It doesn't interest me
where or what or with whom
you have studied.
I want to know
what sustains you
from the inside
when all else falls away.

I want to know
if you can be alone
with yourself
and if you truly like
the company you keep
in the empty moments.

The words we speak

"The six most important words: I admit I made a mistake.
The five most important words: You did a good job.
The four most important words: What is your opinion?
The three most important words: If you please.
The two most important words: Thank you.
The one least important word: I."

—Anonymous

The words we speak set the stage for any of our interactions with ourselves and with others.

When we speak to others in anger, we sometimes mindlessly let out a stream of unkempt words.

We regret speaking them, either instantly, or when we come to our senses.

The words we speak out of anger are mostly spoken out of inner frustration of not being understood. We tend to be extremely critical and tend to let out a volley of harsh, hurtful things.

Likewise, when dealing with ourselves while not using the same degree of anger, we tend to tell ourselves stories. We feed our minds with all the negative statements.

It goes into deep details of why things always go wrong, how we are not good enough, how we never measure up, how we don't deserve whatever comes, or even if we get something, we think it's because we were just lucky and we are not worthy of it. The words we use to describe our experiences inevitably manifests in our lives.

When these recurrent conversations keep happening, we slowly start to believe in them.

We believe all of the lies we speak to ourselves.

We convince ourselves that we are not worthy of anything good and therein lies our problems.

When dealing with others we need to be mindful and conscious of what we speak.

We are dealing with another human who is going through their own journey.

So, we need to be conscious of the words we speak.

If you feel you might say something regretful, leave the place, take a breather and when you are calm, approach the situation or person again.

Being silent is not a weakness. In fact, it's a powerful weapon.

When you know the other person is purposely instigating you or is waiting for you to participate, you never give them the satisfaction of making you stoop to their level.

You calmly go about your work without interacting. You consciously step back in your mind.

You do not feed the negative statements with continuity. Apply the same rules to yourself, too.

When you feel like bombarding yourself with what a rotten person you are, step back and do not give energy to those thought forms.

Mistakes are a part and parcel of human lives and every person tends to commit them. But what is beautiful is we can always pick ourselves back and make a fresh start again. Mistakes can be rectified using love and kindness. Speak to yourself and others with kindness. Kindness heals.

Energy and its significance

"If you want to find the secrets of the universe, think in terms of energy, frequency and vibration." – Nikola Tesla

When you start looking at everything as energy, you will slowly shift your way of thinking, being and your approach towards other beings.

Because everyone is energy. Energy is the way you think, react and respond.

When you spend a lot of time ruminating on the things that are going wrong or worrying you, you exert so much energy in being in a state of fear and unrest. The same applies for positive situations, too.

When you are in a state of happiness, your energies are sky high and you attract more such situations.

The people you meet are a story in themselves, and when you interact, energy exchange tends to happen.

If you are energetically weak, you will automatically absorb everyone's energies which will make you angry, irritated, weak or drained.

Whereas if you are energetically empowered, the energy exchange happening will not affect you, because you will be vibrating in a higher frequency, and hence, other negative influences won't harm you.

You can take care of yourself through physical, mental, emotional and spiritual hygiene.

When you are more mindful and you choose to reject thoughts that no longer align with you, you become empowered.

When you consciously distance yourself from the opinions of others, you become empowered.

When you choose to treat yourself better despite the situations you find yourself in, you are empowered.

Life is always about choices.

You can choose to make whatever decision you want.

But you need to also accept responsibility for it. You cannot blame people for being who they are.

If you think that they brought you unhappiness or misery, you are wrong.

If you are extremely honest, you will find that you always had options.

This excludes cases of extreme trauma of physical, sexual, emotional abuse when the situations are completely out of control. If you have not faced such extreme hardships, you are indeed Blessed.

Life may not be going according to the way you want but who said your way was the only way.

Maybe the universe has something much better in store for you.

Enjoy each day as it unfolds. Take things as they come and don't complicate life with never-ending monologues.

Disassociating with others' opinions

"Don't let someone else's opinion of you become your reality." – Les Brown

We have opinions on a whole lot of things. On how things should be and how they shouldn't.

We are quick to be judgmental. We are also very eager to tell others what we think is the right way of doing things.

But sometimes our opinions hurt people. Especially, sensitive people.

The matter of fact is, deep within, no one wants to know another person's opinion unless it aligns with their thought process.

So, when suggestions are given which don't comply to their liking, their first reaction is a defensive one. People find ways to validate their actions. Automatically, our subconscious triggers an instinctive reaction of either defending ourself, lashing out or silently feeling upset or angry.

How did this even come about?

When you tell people your story, they are automatically going to tell you what they think about it, whether you like it or not. If you are not interested in their opinions, stick to casual conversations and keep your meaningful conversations for the ones you respect and want advice from.

You always have options. If you like someone's advice, you can either accept it, or even better, release it from your mind.

We don't have to spend our energy and time brooding over who said what.

We have the power to choose what thoughts we would like to have.

We disassociate from the opinions that don't improve our life. Not the person. Just their opinion.

We reconsider what we want to share, and with whom. Life is much easier when we stop complicating it.

"Often people that criticise your life are usually the same people that don't know the price you paid to get where you are today. True friends see the full picture of your soul." — Shannon Alder

The strangest secret

"Nurture your mind with great thoughts, for you will never go any higher than you think." – Benjamin Disraeli

This is an excerpt taken from the book 'The Strangest Secret' by Earl Nightingale. This is a lesson we all need to learn and remember to apply in our daily lives.

We become what we think about.

Conversely, the person who has no goal, who doesn't know where he's going, and whose thoughts must therefore be thoughts of confusion, anxiety and worry - his life becomes one of frustration, fear, anxiety and worry. And if he thinks about nothing... he becomes nothing.

How does it work? Why do we become what we think about? Well, I'll tell you how it works, as far as we know. To do this, I want to tell you about a situation that parallels the human mind.

Suppose a farmer has some land, and it's good, fertile land. The land gives the farmer a choice; he may plant in that land whatever he chooses. The land doesn't care. It's up to the farmer to make the decision.

We're comparing the human mind with the land because the mind, like the land, doesn't care what you plant in it. It will return what you plant, but it doesn't care what you plant.

Now, let's say that the farmer has two seeds in his hand- one is a seed of corn, the other is nightshade, a deadly poison. He digs two little holes in the earth and he plants both seeds-one corn, the other nightshade.

He covers up the holes, waters and takes care of the land... and what will happen? Invariably, the land will return what was planted.

As it's written in the Bible, "As ye sow, so shall ye reap."

Remember, the land doesn't care. It will return poison in just as wonderful abundance as it will corn. So up come the two plants - one corn, one poison.

The human mind is far more fertile, far more incredible and mysterious than the land, but it works the same way. It doesn't care what we plant, success or failure. A concrete, worthwhile goal...or confusion, misunderstanding, fear, anxiety and so on. But what we plant must return to us.

You see, the human mind is the last great unexplored continent on earth. It contains riches beyond our wildest dreams. It will return anything we want to plant.

We are all connected

"We cannot live only for ourselves. A thousand fibers connect us with our fellow men; and among those fibers, as sympathetic threads, our actions run as causes, and they come back to us as effects." – Herman Melville

Whether we realize it or not, we impact the lives of the people around us.

To a point that, even without you realizing, people are observing, learning and picking up cues from you.

Your words are being reflected and absorbed. Your actions are being monitored.

How you make someone feel has the greatest impact too.

The world operates on this Universal Law of Connection.

You will hear a friend telling you they were tempted to eat something because they saw you doing it.

Maybe they were inspired to pick up a habit.

To work on themselves. To try something new.

We are not consciously doing anything differently.

We are all connected by these innumerable invisible threads and our presence makes a difference in the lives of those around us.

Live to your greatest potential and those that love, admire and care, will follow you.

They will want to do more, knowing you are there, doing your best every single day.

Live a life of greatness. Lead by example.

This world becomes better by the everyday actions of ordinary people like you and me.

When in love

"Love is a feeling, a feeling of happiness. Love is powerful, too powerful to play with. This feeling is strange and hard to describe, but when you fall in love, you will know it inside." – Unknown

Do you remember the first time you fell in love?

Or the first time you met your significant other?

Do you remember the first time you started interacting with that person?

The profound joy you felt.

The need to talk to this person. The need to make them happy.

The need to do things for them that brought a smile.

Didn't you spend your time and energy in thinking of ways to make them happy?

You made them special dishes and got them gifts.

When there was a discord between you two, an argument or a fight, weren't you always willing to forgive?

You were so much in love that you were able to forgive them for almost anything.

Pleasing them and making them happy seemed to be your goal.

You were willing to be friends with their friends and family.

You wanted to listen to their music and read their books.

You wanted to know every little thing about them.

Their likes and dislikes.

You cried when they felt sad and you laughed at all of their silly stories.

Life was breathtaking knowing they were around.

You couldn't wait to see them, talk to them and be with them.

You were so much in love, giddy with excitement, and you felt safe knowing someone had your back.

Now replace them with you. YOU are that person.

Love yourself unconditionally. Be that special person to yourself.

Complaining in times of calamity

"The world becomes a better place when people get busy doing what they love instead of complaining about what they hate." – Anonymous

It's ok to whine, complain, cry, curse. What is not ok is to wallow in there.

Life will change and we humans actually never learn the lessons.

In the present scenario, there are people who are anxious and worried.

In time, all of this will be behind us and our lives will get back to the routines we are accustomed to and eventually, we will forget about all the hardships we faced.

But I wish we could learn to lead more simpler lives.

That we could eat home cooked meals, spend more time with family and live more economically.

For those who lost loved ones, the impact will be more. For those who lost their jobs, it will be a huge blow.

If we have everything we need to survive and everyone we care about are with us, then we are immensely blessed.

I can only speak from my perspective.

I am not too much of an anxious, worried person.

I am grateful for the innumerable blessings in my life.

I ask myself only two questions; Have I done enough? What more can I do?

I then go about my work.

Life has taught me that happiness comes only from within me.

No one else can make me happy.

It is my responsibility to be in a content state.

Expecting others to make me happy is something I try and avoid.

I do all the things that make me happy, by myself.

Reading, writing, laughing, talking, cooking.

What others think or talk about me, no longer bothers me.

I am extremely happy for every little thing.

And if I should ever pass away any minute, I would be content, knowing I did whatever I possibly could.

This is my wish for every person I meet.

To find inner peace and contentment. To feel secure and safe. To be happy.

I am doing all I can and hope one day all of you dig deep into your inner reserves and know it's absolutely fine to be happy.

How to be happy

"The secret of happiness is not in doing what one likes, but in liking what one does." – James M. Barrie

There are relatively simple ways of being happy.

But unfortunately, for whatever twisted logic in ourselves, we feel we have to be sad, worried or anxious.

Some feel guilty for being happy. Happiness is contagious. Being in a state of happiness attracts more happy situations.

During such difficult times, isn't it wrong to feel happy?

Actually, it is during times like these, that you must step up your Happiness Quotient.

You are not doing the world or anyone a favor if you keep being anxious or panicky.

When you focus on being happy and keeping your family happy, everyone is automatically enveloped in Loving Kindness. Healing begins with each individual.

What can you do to be happy?

Do all of the things you love and things that make you happy.

Do it without feeling guilty. Enjoy all of life's precious gifts.

The breath you take, the family you are surrounded with, the material comforts you have and the food you eat.

Keep everyone and anyone in your prayers.

After that, move on and don't focus on the outside world. Your home and your family are your entire world.

Laugh out aloud as many times as you can. Talk to people who make you happy.

Listen to funny videos. Be creative with your happiness.

It is when you are happy, that you remain healthy.

When you are happy, you radiate happy thoughts and you do yourself and the world a favor.

Every happy thought travels around, and in our own way, we are doing our best to help all those who are putting their lives at risk, ensuring our safety.

Send them waves of happiness.

You will be doing your part in healing the world. Don't let anyone make you feel guilty.

Let happiness radiate from you each being. Your life can be a breathtaking symphony.

Are you on a diet?

"People tend to be generous when sharing their nonsense, fear, and ignorance. And while they seem quite eager to feed you their negativity, please remember that sometimes the diet we need to be on is a spiritual and emotional one. Be cautious with what you feed your mind and soul. Fuel yourself with positivity and let that fuel propel you into positive action." – Steve Maraboli

Have you noticed that sometimes the people around you are extremely quick to jump to conclusions? They are also misguided in their intention to help. This mostly holds true where food is concerned. There is so much tantrum around food related issues. When someone tells you they don't want to eat, you need to respect their boundaries.

Every person's body is unique. What is ok for one may be an allergy for another.

They may genuinely be having health issues and your insensitivity doesn't help them.

The coffee they turn down, the biryani they can't digest or the fruits served at a wrong time can be indicators of what may not be agreeing to their system.

Or maybe on that particular day, they aren't keen on having tempting food or even an extra scoop of ice cream for that matter.

Someone maybe vegan, eggetarian, vegetarian, selective vegetarian or pure non vegetarian.

Don't judge someone based on their choices of food. Sometimes they may be going through a phase of experimentation to figure out what ails them and what heals them.

Respect a person's boundaries and let them find their way. Hold space for them as they find themselves, because what they need right now is your understanding.

Be mindful the next time you mindlessly comment Are you on a diet?

Introspection and conquering our weaknesses

"The most introspective of souls are often those that have been hurt the most." – Shannon Alder

The hardest truth we need to accept is that we are not perfect.

We are filled with faults. We tend to make mistakes.

We tend to project our mistakes on others. It is our weaknesses that makes us falter.

So, if we aren't perfect, what is it that we do.

We learn. We constantly upgrade ourselves. We turn our focus inward rather than spending our energies on the people around us.

We have been put on this earth because we are special. We are unique.

When we heal ourselves, we heal our entire family line. We leave this world a much better place than it was before.

How does one achieve all this?

By being in the moment consciously.

By practicing Gratitude.

By practicing Forgiveness.

By accepting people as they are.

By learning that unwantedly being anxious is never going to get us anywhere.

By always remembering everything begins with us.

It all starts in our minds.

We are more powerful than we ever give ourselves credit for.

When we start working on ourselves, we slowly disintegrate our stuck patterns of living.

We need to do soul searching.

The questions we need to ask ourselves are:

What are my weaknesses? What can I do better? How can I overcome them?

A few examples of weaknesses:

Being extremely sensitive, anxious, getting irritated for the slightest of reasons, having zero tolerance for mistakes, being impatient and quick to judge and draw conclusions, being silent, getting angry, using harsh words, talking incessantly, not speaking up when needed, overdoing, losing the plot, lying, covering up, cheating and never knowing when to say no. It could be anything.

Take a look at them. Analyze how better to improve.

Take help from someone you trust in case you think you can't handle it all. Put your trust in the Divine and seek for guidance.

We need to remember that working on ourselves is the first step to constructive recovery.

Though, these may take time and we may slip up, but it's still better than not trying.

Always keep in mind; healing begins with you. You have the strength within yourself to overcome all your struggles. Remind yourself of that at all times.

Who stole your rainbow?

"God puts rainbows in the clouds so that each of us – in the dreariest and most dreaded moments – can see a possibility of hope." – Maya Angelou

What if I told you no one stole your rainbow?

What if I told you that it is just misplaced?

Would you believe me?

Your rainbow is all your varied skills. Your values, your confidence, your strength and all that makes you shine.

Your rainbow got misplaced while you were distracted and caught up in everydayness. It got misplaced amidst your fears and doubts.

As a tender being, when you are affected by everything that happens to you or when you let others affect you with their words or deeds, you give into hopelessness.

You let others chip away your sparkle and your true essence of being.

You spend your energy in trying to either correct the situation or else spend endless hours ruminating on how situations could have been handled better.

You need to remember the sublime truth that in one's spiritual journey, everyone is on a different path and all of us set a different pace.

While the destination is the same for everyone, the paths you choose are based on the choices you make every day or the things that you comprise yourself with.

It is based on the people you associate with, the books you read, the music you listen to and the lessons you are willing to learn.

You are responsible for every little thing you do. You are answerable for your thoughts, words and actions. You can associate with the right people who bring out the best in you.

You can either choose to be in a state of negativity and anxiety or you can choose to center yourself and find your inner peace.

You can choose to let people dictate the way you need to be, or you can be the better person and choose to forgive people for not behaving better.

You have a choice to be as petty as them by holding grudges for whatever has transpired or you can choose to move along.

You are the choices you make. You need to remember that no one is coming to save you. You need to work on yourself day by day and put in the effort because you know deep down that you are enough.

You can challenge yourself to respond better and you can choose to do things that align with your spiritual self.

You cannot compromise on your values, goodness and character

You need to be excited, bustling with joy, with a sparkle in your eye and a smile on your face.

Rediscover all the things that you love about yourself.

Your Rainbow is waiting to be discovered.

How to handle anxiousness?

"Anxiety does not empty tomorrow of its sorrows, but only empties today of its strength." – Charles Spurgeon

It is reported that more than 90% of what we worry about never happens. That means that our negative worries have less than 10% chance of being correct. If this is so, isn't being positive more realistic than being negative? … If you think about it, the important issue is not which is more realistic, but rather, "Why be miserable when you can be happy?

When we are trapped in situations that cause severe and debilitating anxiousness, we need the coping skills to get through. We need to find the inner peace we seek.

To all those who are anxious, worried or in a state of restlessness, take it day by day, moment by moment.

Remember everything starts in your mind.

Find your center. Find the one thing that gives you immense peace. Do it.

Even if it means retreating to a room and staring into space- do it.

Don't feel guilty for your 'me time'. Don't let anyone make you feel guilty, too.

If you are not up to your full functioning self, it will end up being detrimental for everyone around you. That's why your happiness needs to be your priority.

Anytime you start feeling anxious, stop doing whatever you are doing, immediately.

Take three deep, relaxing breaths. Reaffirm all is well and all will always be well.

Tell your favourite shloka or prayer or affirmation or focus on anything that brings your attention back to this moment.

You will start feeling better. Continue with your work.

Reach out to your family or friends when things overwhelm you.

They will give you a different perspective or reassure you and be the shoulder you need.

Over and above stay away from the media. Don't give in to the need to keep on discussing about how you feel.

While all of this helps immensely, the best way to overcome is to place your entire trust on the Universe.

Trust that the Higher Beings will always take care of you

Do your prayers, meditation, chanting or listen to divine music.

You need to become one with your Higher Self.

Lie down and focus on your breath as you allow your body to relax. Inhale peace and exhale tension.

Deep down, reaffirm yourself that life is good, as you release all the things that weigh you down.

Gossip

"Great minds discuss ideas. Average minds discuss events. Small minds discuss people." – Henry Thomas Buckle

Gossip is a manner of sharing salacious information, often about a person's relationships, love life, or other personal issues that they may not feel comfortable sharing. Usually, gossip involves going into details of some sort, which means the information is shocking or personal. What's more, gossip is usually spoken behind a person's back and can be very hurtful.

When we take time to observe our thoughts, we may come to the understanding that most of our thoughts are mostly repetitive and fixated on what others have said or done to us.

We love glamourizing and recalling the faults of others and take perverse pleasure in magnifying every action of theirs. We spend a lot of our time and energies on meaningless conversations.

We find immense satisfaction in digging up old hurts and past incidents. We portray ourselves as the victim and glorify our smallness while being vindictive of the other person involved.

The more we indulge in such pettiness, the more we attract such situations into our lives.

We need to remember that what happened has happened, and what has to happen, will.

As humans, most of us are guilty of having done this, but this doesn't excuse our continuing willingness to be a partner to such hateful activities. We need to make a conscious effort to bring an end to it.

We don't give in to the temptation to indulge in them or wallow in them. We don't put our energies into discussing it.

If peace is what you seek, set the boundaries and keep yourself in a better space, mentally.

Don't take everything personally

"Don't take anything personally. Nothing others do is because of you. What others say and do is a projection of their own reality, their own dream. When you are immune to the opinions and actions of others, you won't be the victim of needless suffering." – Don Miguel Ruiz

At times when you look back, you realize a lot of unwanted feelings could have been avoided if only you stopped taking everything personally.

Every little thing someone says, is taken as hurt, an insult, an accusation, misconstrued or even looked at as contempt or as a condescending act.

Our egos have become so fragile that everything and anything affects our sensibilities. So, how then, do you overcome this?

Reclaim your power. Stop looking at everything from a victim's perspective.

Don't allow your mind to play tricks on you. Overthinking tends to cause unnecessary pain.

Step back mentally and calmly assess the situation. Let go and embrace the present moment.

If caught in an emotional quagmire, walk away from that space before speaking out words that you will come to regret.

If you are stuck in a place from where you are unable to move, start counting in reverse, take deep breaths, keep looping lyrics from your favourite song or start chanting any mantra and keep at it over and over again.

Give yourself permission to be happy

"When you give yourself permission to communicate what matters to you in every situation you will have peace despite rejection or disapproval. Putting a voice to your soul helps you to let go of the negative energy of fear and regret." – Shannon L. Alder

If you are waiting for permission to live your life, you are never going to get it.

It is not somebody else's responsibility to make you happy. It's yours and yours alone.

Find joy in the smallest of things.

In the breaking of dawn, gurgling of streams, chirping of birds and rustling of trees.

Find joy in the breaking of ocean waves and the sand beneath your feet.

Happiness is all around you. You don't need anyone to validate your feelings.

Be happy, and that too, for no reason, because you intend to.

Be true to yourself

"Be true to yourself. Make each day a masterpiece. Help others. Drink deeply from good books. Make friendship a fine art. Build a shelter against a rainy day." – John Wooden

The person you need to trust the most is yourself
Neither your spouse nor your children
Neither your friends nor your family
But yourself
You need to learn to trust your vibe
The uneasiness you feel
You need to stop making excuses for the toxicity around you
You need to trust yourself when you're being taken for a ride
When you feel suffocated by the double standards you face
When blatant lies and rudeness become a routine
You need to stop confusing yourself that it's your imagination
You need to trust yourself the most
Only when you take a stance for yourself,
will you grow from within
The confidence that you have in yourself
will make you stronger
Don't always rely on others to sort out your mess

Be your own best friend
Know that you are capable of discerning the truth
If someone is messing with your head, give them a wide berth
Your energies are not a playground
You are in a Divine space and you need to trust and remember it at all times.

Life

By Khalil Gibran

Do not love half lovers
Do not entertain half friends
Do not indulge in works of the half talented
Do not live half a life
and do not die a half death
If you choose silence, then be silent
When you speak, do so until you are finished
Do not silence yourself to say something
And do not speak to be silent
If you accept, then express it bluntly
Do not mask it
If you refuse then be clear about it
for an ambiguous refusal is but a weak acceptance
Do not accept half a solution
Do not believe half truths
Do not dream half a dream
Do not fantasize about half hopes
Half a drink will not quench your thirst
Half a meal will not satiate your hunger
Half the way will get you no where
Half an idea will bear you no results

Your other half is not the one you love
It is you in another time yet in the same space
It is you when you are not
Half a life is a life you didn't live,
A word you have not said
A smile you postponed
A love you have not had
A friendship you did not know
To reach and not arrive
Work and not work
Attend only to be absent
What makes you a stranger to them
and them, strangers to you
The half is a mere moment of inability
but you are able for you are not half a being
You are a whole that exists to live a life
not half a life

Bamboo and fern

"Bamboo is flexible, bending with the wind but never breaking, capable of adapting to any circumstance. It suggests resilience, meaning that we have the ability to bounce back even from the most difficult times."
– Ping Fu

One day I decided to quit my job, my relationship, my spirituality… I wanted to quit my life.

I went to the woods to have one last talk with God

"God", I said, "Can you give me one good reason not to quit?".

His answer surprised me… "Look around", He said. "Do you see the fern and the bamboo?

"Yes", I replied.

"When I planted the fern and the bamboo seeds, I took very good care of them.

I gave them light. I gave them water. The fern quickly grew from the earth.

Its brilliant green covered the floor. Yet nothing came from the bamboo seed. But I did not quit on the bamboo.

In the second year, the fern grew even more vibrant and plentiful.

And again, nothing came from the bamboo seed. But I did not quit on the bamboo", he said.

"In year three, there was still nothing from the bamboo seed. But I would not quit.

In year four, again, there was nothing from the bamboo seed. I did not quit" he said.

"Then, in the fifth year, a tiny sprout emerged from the earth. Compared to the fern, it was seemingly small and insignificant…But just 6 months later, the bamboo rose to over 100 feet tall.

It had spent the five years growing roots. Those roots made it strong and provided it with everything that was needed to survive

I would not give any of my creations a challenge it could not handle."

He told me "Did you know, my child, that all this time you have been struggling, you have actually been growing roots?".

"I would not quit on the bamboo. I will never quit on you."

"Don't compare yourself to others." he said. "The bamboo had a different purpose than the fern.

Yet, they both make the forest beautiful." Your time will come", God said to me.

"You will rise high". "How high should I rise?" I asked.

"How high will the bamboo rise?" He asked in return.

"As high as it can?" I answered. "Yes." He said, "Give me glory by rising as high as you can."

The future belongs to those who can rise above the confines of the earth."-Alfred North Whitehead.

What can I do for you?

What can I do for you despite all that you send my way?
My silence may bother you, but silence is not always a weapon.
It is a shield, too. I use it to keep myself safe.
Not because I want to hurt anyone
But because I want to protect myself better.
What can I do for you?
Keep you in my prayers.
You need not know everything and anything about me and neither do I.
But I am always ready and ever willing
to keep you in my prayers.
What can I do for you?
I can always do my best.
I can prove to you and to myself, that my best is yet to come.
Not out of spite but because I now prioritize myself over you.
What can I do for you?
Hold space in my heart.
For a day will come when I will need you, and you, me.
I know my heart is big enough to accommodate us all.

What will it take for you to live life to your fullest potential?

Death.

Carol Rifka Brunt quoted "That's the secret. If you always make sure you're exactly the person you hoped to be, if you always make sure you know only the very best people, then you won't care if you die tomorrow."

The fact that we are mortals and eventually die is something we know, but tend to forget.

But what if you had only this one day?

Maybe 5 or 10 hours, maybe just 24 hours?

What then? What would you do next? It then hits you.

There are so many things and people you aren't bothered about. Neither their pettiness nor their grudges or resentments. Their anger is your least concern.

You gravitate towards the people who love you, value you and make you feel special. You want to give your love to the people who have stood for you while you stood for them.

You choose to experience the goodness life has to offer rather than focusing on things that are draining your energies. Your time is irreplaceable and spending it on guilt, anger or on resentments are counterproductive.

So why wait until you have been given a deadline. Why don't you start today? Why not right now?

We need to remember that life is fragile and death, inevitable, but we must make the most of every day that has been given to us, for that is the most precious of all gifts we ever have.

A great teacher explained it this way: "The trouble with you is that you think you have time." We don't know how much time we have. What would it be like to live with the knowledge that this may be our last year, our last week, our last day? In light of this question, we can choose a path with heart. This excerpt is taken from the book A Path with Heart.

You are not your thoughts

"To realize that you are not your thoughts is when you begin to awaken spiritually". – Eckhart Tolle

The parable of the cow

A monk was walking through the marketplace with his disciples when they saw a man dragging a cow by a rope. The monk asked the man to wait and told his disciples to surround them.

"Let me teach you something," he said. "Tell me, who is bound to whom? Is the cow bound to this man or is the man bound to the cow?"

The disciples replied without hesitation: "Of course the cow is bound to the man. The man is the master, he is holding the rope. The cow has to follow him wherever he goes. The man is the master and the cow, the slave."

"Now, watch this," said the monk, and he took a small knife from his pocket and cut the rope. The cow then ran away from the master, who ran after it.

"Look at what is happening," he smilingly said. "Do you see who the master is?

The cow is not interested at all in this man. In fact, the cow is trying to escape from this man.

The parable of the cow deals with the case of the thoughts in our minds. All the nonsense we carry inside, is not interested in us. We, on the other hand, give it much attention. We love to identify with it and obsess about it until we become its slave.

The reality is, we are NOT our thoughts. We are conscious of them, while they are not conscious of us. They don't sit to think about us and ruin their day and life; they barely even know us. It's actually us who create them. It's us who bring upon the nonsense.

Another significant difference between our Higher Self — as opposed to our ego self — and our thoughts, is that thoughts come and go. They are ephemeral, they are transient, they are temporary; just like the ocean waves, always in motion. We are not. We are temporary only in the physical sense.

Yet, most people identify with their thoughts. They fill their heads with them all the time. Naturally, they go crazy trying to make sense of everything in their world; trying to always be in control — by taming the cow with a rope. Their attachment to their thoughts works like a splinter in their brain which constantly disrupts their inner peace, leaving them unsettled, burdened, and consequently unhappy.

You see, as long as we have thoughts in our brain, separating ourselves from them becomes the path to wisdom and inner peace. Everything changes for the better once the thinker inside our heads is silenced, and instead, we embrace the role of the observer. Because, if you don't master your mind, it will become your master. Or possibly, someone else would do it for you.

As such, the moment we separate ourselves from the thoughts is the moment we'll lose interest in the garbage polluting our heads, and understand the uselessness of our attachment to it. Only then, shall it all start to disappear... just like the cow — it will escape and disappear.

The moral is, we do have the power to let go of unwanted thoughts and achieve peace of mind. For in order to grow, we must let go. There is no other way. Now, cut that rope and set yourself free.

The excuses we always come up with

"What we need to understand is that once we rely on using excuses as a way out, they take a life of their own." – Peter Lopez Jr.

Our mind in less than a fraction of a second, can come up with why things aren't working for us.

Take an example of when you want to release weight.

The excuses your mind comes up with can be any of these:

The weather isn't right. It's hot. It's raining. It's too cold. It's dark. It's sunny.

My family doesn't like it. They don't support me. I'm needed at home.

Work is pending. I had a bad night. I had a long night. I don't have the proper gear.

Exercise isn't for me. What will people say? No matter what I do, there's no difference.

We are very creative with our excuses.

The more we delay, the easier it becomes to convince ourselves why our excuses are valid.

Don't give yourself time to talk yourself out of what you want to do.

Just get going as soon as you decide to.

If you want to walk, run, do Yoga, Pilates or Zumba, get out of bed and get going.

If the weather isn't good, exercise in the comfort of your home.

Learn to adapt and be creative. You can climb stairs or use water bottles as dumbbells.

You can use your walls and chair as props or even do light stretches.

Even if work doesn't permit you to get out, use your office chair and do some bending and rotation exercises. You can plan your day well ahead to get the pockets of time you need. It's all about priorities.

Anything is possible if you set your mind to it. Don't let excuses rule your day and your life.

Mel Robbins said it best in her book The 5 -second rule. **"The 5-second rule is simple. If you have an instinct to act on a goal, you must physically move within 5 seconds or your brain will kill it. …. Hesitation is the kiss of death. You might hesitate for a just nanosecond, but that's all it takes. That one small hesitation triggers a mental system that's designed to stop you. And it happens in less than—you guessed it—five seconds.**

When my mind says 'why?'

"The mind creates the abyss. The heart crosses over it. Love is the bridge." – Stephen Levine

When my mind says 'why?', my heart says 'why not?'

When I dared to tread a slightly different path, I was, and am still riddled with doubts and never-ending questions.

Why can't I just mind my own business? Why do I want to see the people around me happy?

What do I gain from pushing people to better their lives?

It's not that I get compensated monetarily.

Great portions of my time goes into activities that don't exactly concern me.

There are people who have taken my services for granted and then there are those who couldn't be bothered to acknowledge the help they have received.

Why then, do I put in this much of an effort?

Is it for the money? Is it for fame? Is it for respect? The answer is No.

I realized I basically needed to do what I love, only for myself. I need to be my biggest, and at times, my only cheerleader, because if I wait for external validation, I won't progress the way I want and the way I need to. I love being involved and committed to my work. My sense of joy is profound.

And like a rainbow that comes amidst the sun and rains, there are moments when I receive beautiful messages from people telling me that their lives have been enriched because of all that I do, making me persevere, knowing that somehow, in some way, I am making a difference.

Emotional upheaval and rebuilding

"Worrying is carrying tomorrow's load with today's strength- carrying two days at once. It is moving into tomorrow ahead of time. Worrying doesn't empty tomorrow of its sorrow, it empties today of its strength." – Corrie Ten Boom

Your heart palpitates while your brain goes numb.

You are confused and emotionally spent and you cannot outrun this feeling of anxiousness.

Sounds familiar?

At times when faced with difficult situations, or when you happen to deal with difficult people, your emotions outrun logic and clouds your judgement.

How then, does one handle all this?

How does one learn to maintain their sanity?

How does one manage to get out with minimal scars to their soul?

Whenever I am concerned, these are my go-to steps:

I keep turning to all the skills I have accumulated.

I withdraw deep within myself.

I lose myself in my work.

I am completely absorbed in what I do.

I replace my fear with possibility.

I use Affirmations and Mantras.

I become my own best friend.

I wait for my heart rate to return back to normal.

I wait for my anxiousness to subside, which it will.

My fear no longer takes up space and blinds my vision.

I am fine. I know without an iota of doubt that I am divinely guided.

I firmly believe I am a being of wisdom.

I am able to overlook the faults of others knowing that they did only what they could.

I am able to raise myself up.

In love, I find my answers.

In Peace, I find Myself.

The gift of time

"Even though God has given the gift of time to all men equally, it is what each man does with this equal gift of time that determines whether or not he will be great."
– Sunday Adelaja

Time is precious. Gifting your time, even more.

When you gift time, unlike a valuable object, this is something that can never be returned.

You have given away a part of yourself that can never be retrieved. It's lost forever in infinite space.

A rabbi named Hayyim Angel, carries reading material with him whenever he goes to a meeting. When asked Why? He said "Because, according to the Talmud [the Jewish book of law], if someone comes late to a meeting, they are committing the sin of stealing—stealing the time of the person who had to wait for them. And it's the worst kind of stealing because what was taken can never be returned. I don't want to cause anyone to sin. So, I always make sure, if I have to wait for someone, they're never in a position of stealing my time."

It not just about giving time. It's about whom you choose to give it too.

Does the other person respect your time? Do they value you or take you for granted?

Some people have a careless attitude. They think others will be always available and they assume they can ask for whatever favour they want. They don't mind barging into others spaces as long as their needs are prioritized.

If you know of such people, this will resonate with you.

I think whether a person is free or occupied, it's up to them to decide if they want to help someone or not.

We can't demean anyone's job by assuming they have lesser responsibilities or is someone who is still finding their ground. These are not reasons to barge into someone's space.

People may be mentally exhausted and may want time to relax or unwind.

A person will also respond only on the basis of the depth of friendship, relationship and value they have. It's a two-way street, of give respect and take respect.

You can ask someone you value, to come to your rescue only if you have a good, strong relationship.

If you keep using people, they will never turn up, even when you genuinely need them.

So, think twice about how precious time is.

Think about how you want to use it. Think about who deserves your time.

Think if others are worthy of your time and how much of it do they need to occupy.

Think twice before you take anyone's time for granted.

Steve Jobs said "It's really clear that the most precious resource we all have is time."

Focus on what you want, not on what you don't want

"When you focus on lack and scarcity and what you don't have, you fuss about it with your family, you discuss it with your friends, you tell your children that you don't have enough - "We don't have enough for that, we can't afford that" - then you'll never be able to afford it, because you begin to attract more of what you don't have. If you want abundance, if you want prosperity, then focus on abundance. Focus on prosperity. – Lisa Nichols

If you become aware of your thoughts, you will realize that you're spending a fair amount of your time on the things you don't want.

Your looping thoughts could be on what you don't want and where you don't want them to be.

You might be focusing on the respect you deserve from others or the toning down of another's attitude towards you.

You may be overtly focusing on the way some people spoke to you or magnifying their rudeness towards you.

If you really think about it, your list will be an endless litany of complaints against all the wrong doings meted to you over a long period of time.

You are so focused on all that's going wrong and all that is wrong.

Instead, you fail to realize you always have a choice.

A choice of redirecting your thoughts. You can choose to focus on what you want, where you intend to be, focusing on your need to succeed.

You can affirm that you are solely responsible for bringing out the best in you.

You can choose to be friends with anyone you want and you are in a position to understand other's perspective.

You don't indulge in gossip and make productive use of your time.

You know that you are capable of learning new things and are always excited about all that's happening around you.

You are mature enough to understand that, at times, people behave rudely when they go through trying times.

Just a slight change in your thoughts and perspectives, empowers you from being the victim in your story, to be the decision maker.

You no longer focus on what doesn't serve you.

You break away from the habit of focusing on unwanted things

You develop better thinking patterns that are empowering.

Every time you become more conscious, you become more aware of when your thoughts aren't in alignment, and the minute you realize where your thoughts are straying, you have the will to gently bring it back to the present and thereby take your power back.

You center yourself by redirecting and channeling your energies in a constructive way.

Focus on what you want, and you shall start seeing the magic unfold.

Your choices lead the way

"Every choice comes with a consequence. Once you make a choice, you must accept responsibility. You cannot escape the consequences of your choices, whether you like them or not. Attitude is a choice. Happiness is a choice. Optimism is a choice. Kindness is a choice. Giving is a choice. Respect is a choice. Whatever choice you make makes you. Choose wisely." – Roy T. Bennett

Every day when we wake up, we are faced with the decisions we need to make and the choices we have. Every decision and every choice plays an important role in shaping our lives. From the moment we're awake, we need to take decisive actions. A daily run, yoga, meditation, prayers or journaling, it could be scrolling social media or googling. When faced with choices, we do certain activities either consciously or unconsciously, because they have become habits by continuous repetition.

Our choices are not limited to just our everyday activities, but also to our responses. We have choices where anger and irritation are concerned. We can choose to respond harshly and we know it's not because anyone said or did something. It's because anger is deep within you. The angrier you become, the more it becomes a habit. Until it becomes a way of living.

You can choose to overcome your limitations. You can choose to be more aware of the situation.

You can choose to respond mindfully. It is a mindful practice and you can unlearn and relearn all over again. You need to remember that you can never change anybody. How others treat you is their karma, how you respond is yours.

When you focus on yourself and improving your thought process, you suddenly realize you stop giving others the power to upset you with their meanness. While you may not be in a position to distance yourself physically at times, you ought to learn how to safeguard yourself emotionally.

There are a whole lot of people caught up within their own world of misery and resort to lashing and spitefulness, never thinking of the collateral damage they cause. You have a choice of responding or reacting, and your choices will be the defining moment in accelerating healing or hurting. The choice is yours.

The bundle of misery

"Nothing is miserable unless you think it so; and on the other hand, nothing brings happiness unless you are content with it." – Boethius,

Every night a man used to call God, repeating the same prayer.

Repeatedly, he would ask, "Do one favor for me, at least one favor, I have been asking you for this my whole life."

"As far as I can see, I am the most miserable man on earth. Why have you chosen me to be the most miserable?

I am ready to exchange my misery with anybody else, anybody will do — just let me exchange my misery with somebody else.

I don't ask for bliss. Can't you give me only this single opportunity to exchange my misery with somebody else? This is not asking much!"

And one night, in his dream, he realized God had spoken. A great voice came from the heavens, saying, "Gather all of your miseries into bundles and bring them to the temple hall."

The whole town gathers their miseries into big bundles and they bring them. This man is tremendously happy: "So the moment has come! It seems something is going to happen!"

He rushes with his bundle. On the way he, finds others, who are also rushing the same way.

By the time he reaches the temple, he becomes afraid, very afraid, because he sees people are carrying bigger bundles than his.

People that he had always seen smiling, famous people in beautiful clothes, always saying nice things to each other, they were carrying bigger bundles.

He starts becoming a little hesitant on whether to go or not, but he has been praying his whole life, so he says, "Let us see what happens."

When they enter into the temple. The voice says, "Put your bundles around the hall." They put their bundles, and the voice says again, "Now you can choose any bundle that you like."

And the miracle of miracles happens: everybody rushes to their own bundle.

This man, too, rushes so fast towards his own bundle, afraid that if somebody else chooses it, then he will be at a loss.

Everybody has chosen their own bundle, with great relief, and they are all happy, carrying their bundles back to their homes.

Even this man is very happy, for the simple reason that "Who knows what is in the other's bundle?

At least we are aware of our own bundle and what it contains. We know what hand we have been dealt with and we have the abilities to overcome them.

Toxic relationships

A toxic relationship is characterized by dominance, insecurity, self-centeredness and one that makes you feel unsupported, misunderstood, demeaned, or attacked. On a basic level, any relationship that makes you feel worse rather than better can become toxic over time. It damages self-esteem and is energetically draining. This is a relationship where you don't feel comfortable and secure.

Somewhere, sometime or maybe even right now, you have been, or are, in a toxic relationship.

It could be a friend; it could be someone in your family.

Have you been apologizing for your behavior most of the time? Have you been cringing inside?

Are you feeling uncomfortable? Does your heart race every time you come in contact with them? Do you plan every word you say? Do you take the blame despite knowing they are at fault and somehow it now ends up being your mistake?

At times there are some people who rub you the wrong way. From being dominant to being intrusive, they don't give others the space to settle down. They literally turn people off by their behaviour and don't even realise the consequences of their actions and its impact on others.

You need to check in on yourself and do a self-audit. Remember, at all times, you know what's best for you. Your friends and family may not understand what you're going through, but don't let anyone tell you otherwise.

If, for whatever reason you feel distressed, anxious or your mind feels messed up, just trust yourself, trust your instincts and walk away if you need to.

You need to re-evaluate your relationships, set boundaries, and limit your access to such people. You can also, in non-confrontational ways, take a stand for yourself. You can even seek a counsel if you think it's beyond your scope of handling.

You need to prioritize your happiness. Remind yourself that the key to happiness is with you at all times. If you hand it over to someone else, you are never ever going to be happy again.

Pleasing them, trying to live up to their expectations, making them happy at the cost of your peace of mind, all of this will never make you happy. You will lose yourself in trying to find ways to meet their expectations. Your happiness shouldn't come at such high costs. Your mental peace matters. You matter.

Outlook

By Priscilla Leonard

Forget each kindness that you do
As soon as you have done it.
Forget the praise that falls to you
The moment you have won it.
Forget the slander that you hear
Before you can repeat it.
Forget each slight, each spite, each sheer
Wherever you may meet it.

Remember every kindness done
To you, whate'er its measure.
Remember praise by others won
And pass it on with pleasure.
Remember every promise made
And keep it to the letter.
Remember those who lend you aid
And be a grateful debtor.

Remember all the happiness
That comes your way in living.
Forget each worry and distress;
Be hopeful and forgiving.
Remember good, remember truth,
Remember Heaven's above you,
And you will find, through age and youth,
True joys and hearts to love you.

The power of silence

Silence is ever powerful.

Despite all the chaos and turmoil around you, when you choose to be silent, you become empowered.

When the person or people around you don't have the maturity or silence to understand or comprehend you, silence is golden.

You need not necessarily explain yourself at every point, especially to people who are hell bent on misunderstanding your every motive.

Your silence is a sign of your wisdom and acceptance.

You choose to accept them just the way they are.

You choose to get along with your life, knowing your priorities and what matters the most.

Most often, we engage with other people trying to get them to understand our perspectives.

The problem is, sometimes the other person is not mentally ready to accept your thoughts.

Take your power back by disengaging and disconnecting mentally from such people.

Your silence is your ticket to freedom.

Use it to live an empowering life.

The stories you never hear

Behind every smile is a story.

Behind every photo is another one.

Behind every success is a struggle you don't see.

There's more to this than what meets the eyes.

What may seem as bravado, may be the only thing that a person is holding onto.

What seems like giving airs, may be their only validation of themselves.

Maybe they are fighting against the whole world to be in the position they are in.

Maybe their whole world is their family.

Sometimes people are not recognized.

Their talents never appreciated.

They meet with so much ridicule and criticism at every turn, that they slowly become invisible.

So, the next time someone shares something

Go be their biggest cheerleader.

You never know how much you might have made their day.

Appreciation won't cost you anything.

To them, it might just mean the whole world.

Be over the-top generous with your words.

Appreciate more.

Cheer more.

Tell people around you, how much you value them.

Thank them for whatever they do.

It doesn't matter if you do it every day.

Tell them what you think of them.

Let's get all the invisible people to become visible.

Let's get those who hide, to come face the light you have to offer.

You can be the sunshine.

You can be the difference.

It begins with you.

It ends with you.

If I can

St Francis of Assisi

If I can throw a single ray of light across the darkened pathway of another

If I can aid some soul to clearer sight of life and duty, and thus bless my brother

If I can wipe from any human cheek a tear,

I shall not have lived my life in vain while here.

If I can guide some erring one to truth, inspire within his heart a sense of duty

If I can plant within my soul of rosy youth a sense of right, a love of truth and beauty

If I can teach one man that God and heaven are near,

I shall not then have lived in vain while here.

If from my mind I banish doubt and fear, and keep my life attuned to love and kindness

If I can scatter light and hope and cheer, and help remove the curse of mental blindness

If I can make more joy, more hope, less pain,

I shall not have lived and loved in vain.

If by life's roadside I can plant a tree, beneath whose shade some wearied head may rest

Though I may never share its beauty, I shall yet be truly blessed.

Though no one knows my name, nor drops a flower upon my grave

I shall not have lived in vain while here.

Affirmations

"Every time you speak, you are either building up yourself for the better or you are limiting yourself for the worse. Words carry power, therefore before you speak out, speak in... and test your words!"
– Israelmore Ayivor

Affirmations are short, powerful statements that you repeat or reaffirm to yourself. They allow you to consciously be in control of your thoughts. An affirmation is carefully constructed to have the most impact. When you write them, tell them or think them, they become the thoughts that shape your reality. It propels you to get on with the things you want to do. The momentum of positive emotions builds up as soon as you start taking action. Susan Jeffers said "**Every time you encounter something that forces you to "handle it," your self-esteem is raised considerably. You learn to trust that you will survive, no matter what happens. And in this way your fears are diminished immeasurably.**"

Here are a few affirmations one can use.

I give myself permission to heal and grow.

I let go of toxic thoughts.

I release unwanted thoughts.

I am becoming better.

Today, I have chosen to complete my work.

I am choosing kindness.

I choose me.

My life is just the way I want.

I am doing my best.

I will keep doing better than my best.

I am growing and learning every day.

I attract all that is good to me.

I am wise.

I know how to decide.

I will make the correct choices.

I choose to be healthy.

I have a good relationship with what I eat.

I know how to think good thoughts.

I now choose to forgive.

I am going to make myself proud.

I'm freeing myself from all destructive doubt and fear.

I accept myself for who I am and create peace, power and confidence of my mind and heart.

I am going to forgive myself and free myself. I deserve to forgive and be forgiven.

I am healing and strengthening every day.

I've made it through hard times before, and I've come out stronger and better because of them. I'm going to make it through this.

I do not waste away a single day of my life. I squeeze every ounce of value out of each of my days on this planet—today, tomorrow, and every day.

I must remember the incredible power I possess within me to achieve anything I desire.

I do not engage with people who try to penetrate my mind with unhelpful thoughts and ideas—I walk away when a person or a situation isn't healthy for me.

I belong in this world; there are people that care about me and my worth.

My past might be ugly, but I am beautiful inside and out.

I have made mistakes, but I will not let them define me.

My soul radiates from the inside and warms the souls of others.

I don't compare myself to others. The only person I compare myself to is the person I was yesterday. And as long as the person I am today is even the tiniest bit better than the person I was yesterday—I'm meeting my own definition of success.

Desiderata-words for life

— Max Ehrmann, 1927

Go placidly amid the noise and haste,
and remember what peace there may be in silence.
As far as possible without surrender
be on good terms with all persons.
Speak your truth quietly and clearly;
and listen to others,
even the dull and the ignorant;
they too have their story.

Avoid loud and aggressive persons,
they are vexations to the spirit.
If you compare yourself with others,
you may become vain and bitter;
for always there will be greater
and lesser persons than yourself.
Enjoy your achievements as well as your plans.

Keep interested in your own career, however humble;
it is a real possession in the changing fortunes of time.
Exercise caution in your business affairs;
for the world is full of trickery.
But let this not blind you to what virtue there is;
many persons strive for high ideals;
and everywhere life is full of heroism.

Be yourself.
Especially, do not feign affection.
Neither be cynical about love;
for in the face of all aridity and disenchantment
it is as perennial as the grass.

Take kindly the counsel of the years,
gracefully surrendering the things of youth.
Nurture strength of spirit to shield you
in sudden misfortune.
But do not distress yourself with dark imaginings.
Many fears are born of fatigue and loneliness.
Beyond a wholesome discipline,
be gentle with yourself.

You are a child of the universe,
no less than the trees and the stars;
you have a right to be here.
And whether or not it is clear to you,
no doubt the universe is unfolding as it should.

Therefore be at peace with God,
whatever you conceive Him to be,
and whatever your labours and aspirations,
in the noisy confusion of life keep peace with your soul.

With all its sham, drudgery, and broken dreams,
it is still a beautiful world.
Be cheerful.
Strive to be happy.

Our truest freedom comes from our fight from within

"Some of the greatest battles will be fought within the silent chambers of your own soul." – Ezra Taft Benson

"A snake found its way into a carpentry store and as it moved around, it unwittingly slithered over a saw lying on the ground, and was cut. Instinctively, the snake struck out at the saw and bit the tool, seriously wounding its mouth. Not understanding what was happening and believing the saw to be an attacker, the snake decided to wrap its whole body around the saw to constrict and suffocate the supposed enemy. The snake squeezed the saw with all its strength, and in the process wound up killing itself."

Sometimes, we react in anger to hurt those who have harmed us. We believe that they are going to further harm us, and we retaliate, but we do not realize that, we are in fact, hurting ourselves.

As it says in the 20th verse of The Thirty-seven Practices of Bodhisattvas:

As long as you do not subdue the enemy of your own anger,

External foes will only increase as you try to conquer them.

Therefore, calling up the armies of love and compassion,

Subdue your own mind—This is the practice of a bodhisattva.

Within each day, each moment of life, each challenge, adversity and mistake, there's something to be won.

Everything you categorize, or think of as a loss, can be converted into a win. The magic of life is about self-discovery: It's your job to find the wins, to recognize the opportunities for personal growth and to move forward wiser, more self-aware and better prepared for the next battle.

If you focus and concentrate, using the power of your mind, you will set in motion the process of overcoming the things that hold you back. You start to embrace the battles and view them as part of a longer journey— one that will take you to highs, lows and everything in between.

The moment you allow life to drag you down, thinking that there's indefinite amount of time before you can recover, is the moment that you surrender your free will.

To be at peace mentally and emotionally, you often need to be at peace spiritually. This means—you accept life for what it is, acknowledge things at face value, then do your best to influence and impact how you want to change things so they will align with your truth, vision and purpose. It is this vision and purpose that will guide you to win the battle within.

When you try bringing into the spotlight the things that affect you mentally and emotionally, you are able to discern what your priorities are. When you're able to isolate and highlight the things that threaten you, you're better able to analyse and target ways to overcome them. You can dismiss some thoughts as unfitting of your time and move on.

Dedicate a minimum of 10 minutes daily to sort through all that you're facing. It will not be sufficient to solve your problems, but when you sit with yourself, you are preparing yourself mentally and emotionally for each part of your day and you'll become more resilient for approaching any new and old obstacles.

"The battles that count aren't the ones for gold medals. The struggles within yourself, the invisible, inevitable battles inside all of us, that's where it's at." -Jesse Owens"

Success is not in your failure, it's in your 'never say die' attitude

C.S Lewis quoted "You can't go back and change the beginning but you can start where you are and change the ending."

If you are stuck at a cross road, regretting your life choices, or if you feel you have reached a dead-end, always remember, no matter what, you can't change what has happened.

But YOU can start from where you are, analyze, learn, apologize, strategize, brain storm, associate, communicate or do whatever it takes to get you back on course.

Remember Dr. Robert Schuller said "Success is never ending; failure is never final."

Let's talk about improvising. Yes, you are stuck, but likewise you can get unstuck too.

You just need to figure out the right tools to apply. If a relationship is not flourishing, you need to communicate better and make yourself understood. If it requires you to distance yourself, so be it. You apply your judgment and do the needful.

Likewise, in case of a financial crisis, what is it that you can do? Are there people you can talk to? What are the practically doable solutions you can adopt? Are there people you can approach to help you tide over the situation?

Sometimes it's not monetary help that you need, but the strength that comes from knowing that someone out there has your back.

The lesson you need to learn, is not to hold onto the past, but to figure out ways to make your future a brighter one. You need to remind yourself of your greatness and all of your accomplishments.

Don't wait for motivation, high energy, or a sense of focus before taking action. Create motivation by taking action. Once initiated, action tends to gather momentum—tasks become increasingly easy to sustain.

Your success story is waiting to be written. A new one every time.

To thine own self be true

"I do not exist to impress the world. I exist to live my life in a way that will make me happy." – Richard Bach.

We cannot pour from an empty cup, and unless we take care of ourselves, prioritize our needs and be joyous, we won't be able help those who need us.

As a race, we have forgotten how to be happy. We are misguided in thinking that placing the needs of others before us is necessary, sacrificial and rewarding.

It can be, but it comes at great personal costs. Unless and until anything is done with profound peace and joy, all it causes within us, is disharmony.

We are at war with ourselves to maintain peace amongst others.

My personal experiences taught me to take a stand for what I truly believe in. To do all that I do with passion and with grace. To be present for others and to be present for myself.

I learnt that I cannot please everyone, and me being miserable was too big a price to pay.

The value of the lives of the people I enrich and the value of my life in turn being enriched is what I aspire to do.

In living my life to my best potential, I live a more purposeful life.

I learnt that it is both vital and necessary" to thine own self, be true."

Don't quit

by Edgar A. Guest

When things go wrong, as they sometimes will,
When the road you're trudging seems all uphill,
When the funds are low and the debts are high,
And you want to smile but you have to sigh,
When care is pressing you down a bit -
Rest if you must, but don't you quit.

Life is queer with its twists and turns.
As everyone of us sometimes learns.
And many a fellow turns about when he
Might have won had he stuck it out.
Don't give up though the pace seems slow -
You may succeed with another blow.

Often the goal is nearer than it seems
To a faint and faltering man;
Often the struggler has given up when he
Might have captured the victor's cup;
And he learned too late when the night came down,
How close he was to the golden crown.

Success is failure turned inside out -
The silver tint of the clouds of doubt,
And when you never can tell how close you are,
It may be near when it seems afar;
So stick to the fight when you're hardest hit -
It's when things seem worst,
You must not quit.

What can't be taken away from you

"Forces beyond your control can take away everything you possess except one thing, your freedom to choose how you will respond to the situation." – Viktor E. Frankl

There are some things that no one can take away from you. These are your most precious assets. Things like your uniqueness, individuality, your character, self-worth, personality, your passions, your transparency, your very essence and your whole existence. Work on them. Let your uniqueness be the definition of who you are.

There is an old story about a famous rabbi living in Europe who was visited one day by a man who had travelled by ship from New York to see him.

The man came to the great rabbi's dwelling, a large house on a street in a European city, and was directed to the rabbi's room, which was in the attic.

He entered to find the master living in a room with a bed, a chair, and a few books. The man had expected much more.

After greetings, he asked, "Rabbi, where are your things?" The rabbi asked in return, "Well, where are yours?" His visitor replied, "But, Rabbi, I'm only passing through," and the master answered, "So am I, so am I."

To love fully and live well requires us to recognize finally that we do not possess or own anything—our homes, our cars, our loved ones, not even our own body. Spiritual joy and wisdom do not come through possession but rather through our capacity to open, to love more fully, and to move and be free in life.

Learn to let go

"To let go does not mean to get rid of. To let go means to let be. When we let be with compassion, things come and go on their own." – Jack Kornfield.

Letting go and moving through life from one change to another brings the maturing of our spiritual being. In the end we discover that to love and let go can be the same thing.

Both ways do not seek to possess. Both allow us to touch each moment of this changing life and allow us to be there fully for whatever arises next.

If you want to lead a life to your truest potential, you need to let go of:

self-doubt and self-criticism
Fear of failing and fear of taking a chance
Procrastination and giving excuses
Feeling entitled and waiting for others to help you
Seeking short cuts and giving in to mediocrity
Closed thinking and stubbornness.

This is an exercise you can try and has been recommended by Jeff Foster, author of **The Way of Rest** He said "If you feel sad or afraid, or feel a tension in your body, just for a moment stop trying to "let go." Forget about "raising your vibration" too! Instead, simply be with the discomfort. Get curious about it. Soften around it. Breathe into it. Give it space, room, some time. Forget about understanding, "releasing," or "fixing" it today and just allow it to be here for as long as it needs to be here. Let it stay if it wants to stay. Let it go if it wants to go! Let it come back if it wants to come back. Treat it like a welcome guest in the vast rest home of your being, a beloved child that truly belongs."

Reclaim your power

"Daring to set boundaries is about having the courage to love ourselves even when we risk disappointing others." – Brene Brown

Boundaries are a way to take care of ourselves. It is about respecting yourself enough to take a stand for yourself.

When there are no clear boundaries, we send a signal that we are okay with what's happening to us and that we are unwilling to create a scene or fight. You wave the green flag of acquiescing, silently tolerating whatever happens to you.

Not having a boundary makes you a doormat with a welcome sign that says, 'please step on me I will take whatever you dish out to me.'

Setting boundaries is more about loving yourself enough. It is about nurturing and prioritizing yourself, thereby making room for self-respect and self-love.

You need to remember you aren't punishing anyone. You are safeguarding your space.

You are reclaiming your power and, in the process, loving yourself more.

Value yourself enough to know what your boundaries are and trust your judgement when you define them to yourself and to others. Never let it be about them.

When you understand how to set and maintain healthy boundaries, you can avoid the feelings of resentment, disappointment, and anger that build up when limits have been pushed.

"Love yourself enough to set boundaries. Your time and energy are precious and you get to decide how you use them. You teach people how to treat you by deciding what you will and won't accept." —Anna Taylor

Looping thoughts

"Thoughts are only thoughts. They are not you. You do belong to yourself, even when your thoughts don't."
– John Green

Looping thoughts are the persistent thoughts that repeatedly run through your head, 24/7, literally like a broken track. No matter what you do, it doesn't go away because your mind is now invaded by aliens.

The aliens are your looping thoughts. Looping thoughts can be extremely deceptive. They creep upon you when you are at your weakest, attack you, shatter your defences completely and then control the way you think.

Once caught up in the cesspool of a looping thought, it becomes the only way you think. You are now on auto pilot. Outwardly, you will be functioning normally, no one other than you will know that you have been attacked by them and while you keep going about your daily life, you know you are being strangled from within. You have no way of coming out.

If this is something you identify with, you must remember that looping thoughts are aliens, and like all aliens, they can be destroyed. You can take away their powers. But this requires patience, persistence and discipline to fight a good fight.

Looping thoughts think they are smart, so they keep calling the shots. Once you become aware of your looping thoughts, you start calling them out. It may seem silly, but it isn't so. You talk to your thoughts. Remind yourself you are Not Your Thoughts. That this is just a figment of your imagination.

Start engaging in productive tasks. Listen to music that uplifts you. Associate with people who understand and support you. Take professional help when required. Break down and have a good cry if needed and flush it out of your system.

Give yourself time. Time is the biggest healer. Mistakes are bound to happen as you fall back on repetitive behavioural patterns, but remind yourself to get back up and keep trying. As you keep on working on yourself, you will notice that the hold that looping thoughts had over you has now loosened.

It will make its presence felt when it comes across cues of old memories, but you can be confident that those are reality checks to assure you that you have won this round and you will survive again.

Are you holding onto guilt?

"Maybe there's more we all could have done, but we just have to let the guilt remind us to do better next time." – Veronica Roth

Are you blaming yourself for a failed relationship?
For being rude and harsh
For a wrong business decision
For your child messing up
For your inability to conquer your weaknesses
For binge watching your favourite show
For all those late nights you stay up
For the mindless scrolling on your phone
For that extra cigarette you smoked
For the chocolate you sneaked in
For the exercises you skipped
For the doctor's visit you postponed
For the calls you didn't make
For the relationships you refuse to forgive
For your inability to move on
For your fears and shames

Do not feel guilty
You are not perfect…… Yet

This is a journey of self-discovery and learning.

You are trying, and even if you aren't, you need to give yourself a chance to do better and be better.

Feeling guilty will only strangle you, and only when you consciously take proactive steps, would you have a chance of improving yourself.

When you do self-reflection, you need to remember that you are not that person anymore. When you started out, you didn't have the wisdom and maturity you have now. That's why guilt is counterproductive. Forgive yourself for not knowing better. Be determined to consciously work towards your self-improvement. Going forward is the only way.

"There are two kinds of guilt: the kind that drowns you until you're useless, and the kind that fires your soul to purpose." — Sabaa Tahir

Thank you

"In ordinary life, we hardly realize that we receive a great deal more than we give, and that it is only with gratitude that life becomes rich." – Dietrich Bonhoeffer

Having an attitude of gratitude has been one of my biggest lessons. It turned my life around and opened the doors to living a life filled with bliss.

Being in gratitude is now my way of living.

Thank You is a word I use as easily as I breathe.

I truly don't need any special day to express my gratitude.

I am grateful for each and every little possession I own and for every act of kindness I receive.

I am grateful for my family and friends.

I am extremely grateful to the people who weren't nice to me. They helped me turn my life around and taught me some much-needed lessons.

I am in gratitude for all of my material comforts and for all of the things I normally tend to take for granted.

I am in gratitude for my mentors who are beacons of hope, guiding my path.

I am grateful for all the lessons and opportunities that come my way.

I am in gratitude for the love I receive and for the love I give.

I am in gratitude to those who believe in me and make me believe in myself.

I am grateful to nature for the abundance and to the Universe for having my back.

Eckhart Tolle quoted "Acknowledging the good that you already have in your life is the foundation for all abundance".

Conclusion

Dearest Reader

In my quest to understand myself better, I learnt my lessons the hard way. When my goodness was tested, my integrity questioned and my innate kindness taken for granted, I was left with questions and agonizing pain for not having any answers. Why do people treat others a certain way? Can rudeness be a way of living? Can we hurt someone callously?

When a person is naïve, it is automatically perceived as a weakness. We are told to be stronger, to fight back, stand our ground, or at times even asked to be discourteous.

But what if this is against your very nature? What if you are a peace-loving, calm, kind person.

How, then, does one handle this?

My lessons came when I realized that "We do not see things as they are. We see things as we are".

My naivety makes me trust people. My kindness makes me extend help.

My thoughtfulness extends to all beings, irrespective of how they are.

With clarity came the understanding, I am Who I am.

My naivety, kindness and thought processing set the tone for my interactions and define who I am.

I cannot stoop down to meet someone who doesn't rise up to meet me.

My perspectives give me clarity to focus on only those whom matter.

I realized it is imperative to live a significant life, wherein we leave footprints worth following.

Every one of us is unique and no one can ever replicate us.

I am reminded of this short story, which I hope restores your faith in yourself.

There was a man who made living selling balloons at a fair. He had all colours of balloons, including red, yellow, blue, and green. Whenever business was slow, he would release a helium-filled balloon into the air and when the children saw it go up, they all wanted to buy one. They would come up to him, buy a balloon and his sales would go up again. He continued this process all day. One day, he felt someone tugging at his jacket. He turned around and saw a little boy who asked, "If you release a black balloon, would that also fly?" Moved by the boy's concern, the man replied with empathy, "Son, it is not the colour of the balloon; it is what is inside, that makes it go up."

The same thing applies to our lives. It is what is inside, that counts. **The thing inside of us that makes us go up, is our attitude.**

I hope that each of you realize this for your own selves. You are valuable and you deserve better at all times. When life treats you badly, do not respond with bitterness. Instead, choose to be in alignment with your true purpose of being divine. There is beauty in riding life's cosmic waves of experiences and learning the lessons intended.

Quotations

As a reader, I have always loved quotations. I love reading and reflecting on them, for they make me think from a completely different perspective. Quotations are those quick 'pick me ups'. An instant energy booster. Every time you feel down, all you need to do is go through them. These have been handpicked for a purpose. I hope they make you feel better every time you go through them. They have been placed at the end for a reason. You can always come back to these pages every time you need hand holding and solace for your mind.

"Life is amazing. And then it's awful. And then it's amazing again. And in between the amazing and awful it's ordinary and mundane and routine. Breathe in the amazing, hold on through the awful, and relax and exhale during the ordinary. That's just living heart breaking, soul-healing, amazing, awful, ordinary life. And it's breathtakingly beautiful."

– L.R. Knost

"If you deliberately plan on being less than you are capable of being, then I warn you that you'll be unhappy for the rest of your life."

– Abraham Maslow

"Words have a magical power. They can bring either the greatest happiness or deepest despair; they can transfer knowledge from teacher to student; words enable the orator to sway his audience and dictate its decisions. Words are capable of arousing the strongest emotions and prompting all men's actions."

– Sigmund Freud

"Be who you are and say what you feel, because those who mind don't matter, and those who matter don't mind."

– Bernard M. Maruch

"Once you start making the effort to 'wake yourself up'—that is, be more mindful in your activities—you suddenly start appreciating life a lot more."

–Robert Biswas-Diener

"Do not be dismayed by the brokenness of the world. All things break. And all things can be mended. Not with time, as they say, but with intention. So, go. Love intentionally, extravagantly, unconditionally. The broken world waits in darkness for the light that is you."

– L.R. Knost

"Beliefs have the power to create and the power to destroy. Human beings have the awesome ability to take any experience of their lives and create a meaning that disempowers them or one that can literally save their lives."

– Tony Robbins

"Too often, we fall into an all-or-nothing cycle with our habits. The problem is not slipping up; the problem is thinking that if you can't do something perfectly, then you shouldn't do it at all."

– James Clear

"Never neglect the little things. Never skimp on that extra effort, that additional few minutes, that soft word of praise or thanks, that delivery of the very best that you can do. It does not matter what others think, it is of prime importance, however, what you think about you. You can never do your best, which should always be your trademark, if you are cutting corners and shirking responsibilities. You are special. Act it. Never neglect the little things."

– Og Mandino

"These are the few ways we can practice humility:
To speak as little as possible of one's self.
To mind one's own business.
Not to want to manage other people's affairs.
To avoid curiosity.
To accept contradictions and correction cheerfully.
To pass over the mistakes of others.
To accept insults and injuries.
To accept being slighted, forgotten and disliked.
To be kind and gentle even under provocation.
Never to stand on one's dignity.
To choose always the hardest."

– Mother Teresa

"Boundaries define us. They define what is me and what is not me. A boundary shows me where I end and someone else begins, leading me to a sense of ownership. Knowing what I am to own and take responsibility for gives me freedom. Taking responsibility for my life opens up many different options. Boundaries help us keep the good in and the bad out. Setting boundaries inevitably involves taking responsibility for your choices. You are the one who makes them. You are the one who must live with their consequences. And you are the one who may be keeping yourself from making the choices you could be happy with. We must own our own thoughts and clarify distorted thinking."

– Henry Cloud

"Here's to the bridge-builders, the hand-holders, the light-bringers, those extraordinary souls wrapped in ordinary lives who quietly weave threads of humanity into an inhumane world. They are the unsung heroes in a world at war with itself. They are the whisperers of hope that peace is possible. Look for them in this present darkness. Light your candle with their flame. And then go. Build bridges. Hold hands. Bring light to a dark and desperate world. Be the hero you are looking for. Peace is possible. It begins with us."

– L.R. Knost

What you make of life is up to you.
You have all the tools and resources you need
What you do with them is up to you
The choice is Yours.
Stay mindful of your Choices.

To help others live a better life you don't focus on their problems.
You focus on positive solutions that provide a better way for them to live.

"We do not become healers.
We came as healers. We are.
Some of us are still catching up to what we are.
We do not become storytellers.
We came as carriers of the stories we and our ancestors actually lived. We are.
Some of us are still catching up to what we are.
We do not become artists. We came as artists. We are.
Some of us are still catching up to what we are.
We do not become writers... dancers... musicians... helpers... peacemakers.
We came as such. We are. Some of us are still catching up to what we are.
We do not learn to love in this sense.
We came as Love. We are Love. Some of us are still catching up to who we truly are."

– Clarissa Pinkola Estés

"In life no one will remember how you looked, walked, talked or what you did... Everyone will remember you by the way you made them feel when they were with you."

– A. P. J. Abdul Kalam

"A mind is like a parachute. It doesn't work if it is not open."

– Frank Zappa

"It's more selfless to act happy. It takes energy, generosity, and discipline to be unfailingly light-hearted. Yet everyone takes the happy person for granted."

– Gretchen Rubin

"Beyond the edge of the world there's a space where emptiness and substance neatly overlap, where past and future form a continuous, endless loop. And, hovering about, there are signs no one has ever read, chords no one has ever heard."

– Haruki Murakami.

"Champions don't do extraordinary things. They do ordinary things, but they do them without thinking, too fast for the other team to react. They follow the habits they've learned."

– Charles Duhigg

"There comes a time in your life, when you walk away from all the drama and people who create it. You surround yourself with people who make you laugh. Forget the bad and focus on the good. Love the people who treat you right, pray for the ones who do not. Life is too short to be anything but happy. Falling down is a part of life, getting back up is living."

– José N. Harris

"Do the things that interest you and do them with all your heart. Don't be concerned about whether people are watching you or criticizing you. The chances are that they aren't paying any attention to you. It's your attention to yourself that is so stultifying. But you have to disregard yourself as completely as possible. If you fail the first time then you'll just have to try harder the second time. After all, there's no real reason why you should fail. Just stop thinking about yourself."

– Eleanor Roosevelt

"Though fairy tales end after ten pages, our lives do not. We are multi-volume sets. In our lives, even though one episode amounts to a crash and burn, there is always another episode awaiting us and then another. There are always more opportunities to get it right, to fashion our lives in the ways we deserve to have them. Don't waste your time hating a failure. Failure is a greater teacher than success."

– Clarissa Pinkola Estés

"Forgiving does not erase the bitter past. A healed memory is not a deleted memory. Instead, forgiving what we cannot forget creates a new way to remember. We change the memory of our past into a hope for our future."

– Lewis B. Smedes

"When we tackle obstacles, we find hidden reserves of courage and resilience we did not know we had. And it is only when we are faced with failure do, we realise that these resources were always there within us. We only need to find them and move on with our lives."

– A. P. J. Abdul Kalam

"When you produce a thought that is full of understanding, forgiveness, and compassion, that thought will immediately have a healing effect on both your physical and mental health and on those around you. If you think a thought that is full of judgment and anger, that thought will immediately poison your body and mind and the people around you."

– Thich Nhat Hanh

"The Old Irish Healer to the Soul"
It's not your back that hurts, but the burden.
It's not your eyes that hurt, but injustice.
It's not your head that hurts, it's your thoughts.
It's not the throat, but what you don't express or say with anger.
It's not the stomach hurts, but what the soul does not digest.
It's not the liver that hurts, it's the anger.
It's not your heart that hurts, but love.
And it is love itself that contains the most powerful medicine.

(Unknown Author)

"You are not a victim. You are a willing participant that has created your own anxiety through your negative mind, insecurities and actions. If you want to secure your future then the only way is through love, forgiveness and the willingness to admit you have participated in the uncomfortableness you are experiencing now. Stop telling yourself you are justified in hate, indifference, silence or bias. You are not. You can't build a positive life through battling others. The world is full of victims. No one wants to hear that story. People want to know how you did what the majority wouldn't do-you forgave and built up your enemies. It seems totally rare and unheard of these days to swallow your pain and take the high road, but guess what? Those are the leaders that people admire and want to know. Those are the 1% who change the world and people's lives. So why do you want to be like the world when you can be beyond it?"

– Shannon L. Alder

"I will greet this day with love in my heart. And how will I do this? Henceforth will I look on all things with love and be born again. I will love the sun for it warms my bones; yet I will love the rain for it cleanses my spirit. I will love the light for it shows me the way; yet I will love the darkness for it shows me the stars. I will welcome happiness as it enlarges my heart; yet I will endure sadness for it opens my soul."

– Og Mandino

"Sometimes we need a bridge and sometimes we are the bridge. No one I know has escaped troubled waters, rough seas and challenging, scary days. There are times in our lives when we could use a little help, and other times when we are given the chance to be that help for someone else. It really doesn't matter where you are right now. What matters is that you remember we are stronger together, and taking a hand is just as important as offering one."

- Paul Boynton.

About the Author

Danusha Chandrasekaran is the founder of Serenity E-Magazine and author of Have you found your happy place. She has a Master's degree in Human Development & Family Studies and certified courses in alternative therapies. She is a seeker, dreamer and a voracious reader. Having a passion for reading and research helped her lay the foundation to spread positivity through the written word. Experience and real time healing taught her that people could heal themselves. Every person deserves happiness and it is one of her missions to help people realize it for themselves.